THROUGH THE EYES
OF CHRISTMAS

THROUGH THE EYES OF CHRISTMAS

Keys to unlocking the Spirit of Christmas in Your Heart

Ron Davis

ELM HILL

A Division of
HarperCollins Christian Publishing

www.elmhillbooks.com

Through the Eyes of Christmas
Keys to unlocking the Spirit of Christmas in Your Heart

Published in Nashville, Tennessee, by Elm Hill, an imprint of Thomas Nelson. Elm Hill and Thomas Nelson are registered trademarks of HarperCollins Christian Publishing, Inc.

Elm Hill titles may be purchased in bulk for educational, business, fund-raising, or sales promotional use. For information, please e-mail SpecialMarkets@ ThomasNelson.com.

Scripture quotations marked KJV are from the King James Version. Public domain.

Library of Congress Cataloging-in-Publication Data
Library of Congress Control Number: 2018933344

ISBN 978-1-595540287 (Paperback)
ISBN 978-1-595540799 (Hardbound)
ISBN 978-1-595540928 (eBook)

CONTENTS

FOREWORD

In this narrative, Ron Davis examines Christmas from the eyes of those who personally witnessed it: Mary, Joseph, the shepherds and the wise men. His purpose is to uncover the basic Christian principles that inspire the true joy of Christmas in the hearts of those who experience it. In this theme, Christmas is more than an annual holiday celebration: it is a life-changing event that occurs repeatedly in the lives of those who spiritually witness the birth of Jesus Christ in their hearts.

Importantly, the book does more than explain the significance and benefits associated with Christ's coming to the earth. It also expounds on the benefits of experiencing Christ daily in an individual's life so the present world can be a more fulfilled and joyful existence. This volume explains substantial biblical principles, but more significantly the reader will obtain practical tools for making Christmas a continuous life-changing, every-day reality. There is a deep religious hunger in the world today, and Davis explains that the Christmas story is a soul-satisfying experience rather than a theological or philosophical argument. In reading these chapters, one returns to the historical event and joins with those who experienced Christ originally.

Essentially, the narrative takes the reader back to the initial revelation of Christ to the world. Then Davis uses illustrations to describe the distractions of Christmas involving various types of interferences such as the secularization of the blessed and holy event. He also explains distractions resulting from doing the good deeds for a successful Christmas while forgetting the most important aspect of the occasion. For example, laboring to prepare for Christmas but forgetting to worship fully, give joyfully, and share gladly the news of Christ's coming to the world.

In this book, one learns it is impossible to live a successful Christian life without a clear-cut understanding and experience of the most basic Christian principles revealed in the incarnation story. The book concludes with a declaration that the true joy of Christmas is found when one accepts the miracle of Christmas by faith.

Terry Minter, Ph.D.
Professor, Bible/Theology

PREFACE

How do you get into the Christmas spirit? Each December, I face that same question as I prepare to teach my Sunday school class. I want to give my class something that will inspire them, something that will cause them to discover the spirit of Christmas in their lives each year. But how? What are the keys to unlocking Christmas Spirit?

Pastors must ask that same question as they prepare their Christmas sermons. What are they going to say that is inspired, anointed, and will make a real difference in the lives of their parishioners? And those parishioners are wondering what their pastor is going to say to get them in the Christmas spirit so they can enjoy, rather than just endure, the season (and their relatives).

As I studied the Christmas story, it wasn't long before I began to discover that the secret to finding Christmas spirit lay in the lives of the first Christmas participants. Of course, Christmas had not been invented yet for Mary and Joseph. They were preparing for the arrival of Mary's firstborn son—the Son of God.

But everything that we celebrate at Christmas truly begins with the arrival of Jesus in our lives, so there must be something in their lives from which we can discern Christmas spirit.

Listening to coworkers and friends, I heard the disappointment in their voices as we talked about Christmas. Without Jesus in their celebration their Christmas was mostly about family, and if their family was gone (or estranged), what was the point? It really is true: if all we do is pull out the same decorations, put up the same tree in the same corner, with the same wreath on the same front door, we will get the same result—no lasting Christmas joy. Their disappointment is that you can do Christmas things but still fail to see Christmas spirit in your heart.

So I began to study Christmas through the eyes of the first Christmas story participants. What were they focused on that first Christmas and what do their lives teach us about finding the true spirit of Christmas in our own? Year after year I taught a new Christmas lesson with a new revelation of Christmas spirit. It wasn't long before newer members of the class heard about previous Christmas lessons and wanted me to reteach those to them. But as you can imagine, there is just never enough time to go back and teach all of those lessons, so the idea of the book was born.

At its heart, *Through the Eyes of Christmas* is a series of Christmas Sunday school lessons (or if you prefer, Christmas sermons) that redirect our focus at Christmas. It reveals keys to unlocking the true spirit of Christmas in your heart by looking through the eyes of the first Christmas story participants.

But did you know Christmas is more than just Mary, Joseph, Jesus and the manger? There are shepherds who teach us about the joy of Christmas spirit when we share that message with others. There are wise men who teach us about worshipping which ushers in Christmas spirit. There are Simeon and Anna, who teach us you are never too old for Christmas. And since I teach an adult Sunday school class with many senior saints, that is one of their favorite Christmas lessons. There is Jairus, the ruler of the Capernaum synagogue who teaches us how to believe in Christmas. And let's not forget Zachariah and Elizabeth who were expecting Christmas. You will just have to read that chapter to find out why.

Then there is that needful thing: Christmas dinner. And that lesson I learned from my beautiful wife. Like Martha's *cumbered about with much doing*, our Christmas morning had slipped away, the guests for Christmas dinner would soon be here, and my wife was busy trying to do too much in the kitchen by herself. Yes, it was time to stop playing with the toys and help. The needful thing that Christmas was to help her bring the Christmas feast to the table so everyone, especially the cook, could enjoy the celebration of Jesus' coming.

So go grab a cup of coffee, or tea, or hot chocolate, find your favorite chair, sit down and join me on a journey back into the lives and thoughts of Mary, Joseph, the shepherds, the innkeeper, wise men, and a few other specially placed "Christmas" people. As we look *Through the Eyes of Christmas,* we will discover the Biblical truths to birth in our hearts the true, lasting joy that comes with the spirit of Christmas. And when we are done you too will know how to *keep Christmas well.*

Ron Davis

CHAPTER 1

KEEPING CHRISTMAS WELL

"Scrooge was better than his word...and it was always said of him, that he knew how to keep Christmas well, if any man alive possessed the knowledge."

CHARLES DICKENS

Ebenezer Scrooge. Fiction? Of course. But, what about keeping Christmas well? Is that also fantasy or perhaps just unachievable idealism? The idea of keeping Christmas well may cause some to echo Scrooge's familiar refrain: "Bah, humbug!"

But I do love the feeling of joy that comes especially at Christmas. This Christmas spirit is not the secularized concept that the television advertisers have of Christmas. Nor is it the merchandised, tinsel-wrapped idea the retailers want to sell you. Christmas spirit is a lasting joy birthed in faith when you choose to believe in the true spirit of Christmas.

The true spirit of Christmas is not some ghostly visitation that appeared to Ebenezer Scrooge. The true spirit of Christmas is an indescribable joy that emanates from deep within you. It starts when you accept the true meaning of Christmas and apply it to your heart. It is an inexplicable peace that floods your soul and like a rising tide lifts your spirit, regardless of the chaos or confusion that may surround your everyday life.

When you keep Christmas well, the spirit of Christmas changes your attitude; it bubbles up from within you and puts a smile on your face and a spring in your step–especially at Christmas time. It is commonly seen during the month of December on the faces of those who believe. But the real truth is that the true spirit of Christmas is a gift that can be carried with you throughout the year.

Whether we will admit it to ourselves or not, we all yearn for that true spirit of Christmas in our hearts and homes each year. We truly wish our Christmas to be one of peace on earth and goodwill towards men just like the angel announced to the shepherds. But after the shopping, spending, decorating, wrapping and relatives, many times our Christmas experience is far from peaceful and there is little goodwill to go around.

And each Christmas season, we promise ourselves that this year will be different. This year we will have a perfect Christmas with true Christmas spirit. The problem, of course, is how do you find that perfect spirit of Christmas? And once it is found, how do you keep from losing it?

Think back for a moment to your best Christmas memory as a little child. Do you remember those Christmas feelings of awe and anticipation that you had? Deep inside, we all long to recapture the innocence and wonder we felt as a little child at Christmas. But how can you experience that again? How can you experience the real joy of the Christmas season?

I am not talking about that feeling of fleeting happiness that some equate with Christmas joy. I want the joy that infects the true spirit of Christmas. I want an everlasting joy that gives true meaning to Christmas and carries you throughout the year. I want the kind of joy that keeps Christmas well.

It is easy to let the hustle and bustle that accompanies Christmas drown out the Christmas carol we hear in our heart. The *Jingle Bell* march toward a secular Christmas seems to have become the standard. Retailers use Christmas to balance their books for the year. To the retailer, Christmas is just another shopping season for selling. And each year, they seem to start the selling earlier. It is no longer just the day after Thanksgiving that the selling begins; no, now the super-duper, six-hour-only sales start Thanksgiving evening. For many merchants, the Christmas trees, lights, and decorations go up the day after Halloween!

Regrettably, far too many people will buy the secularized

version of Christmas that the retailers sell them. Far too many people will just settle for the same old Christmas. They will 'do' Christmas as they have done in years past. No real, lasting Christmas joy will abound in their heart. They have no true understanding of why we are celebrating the season. They will *do*, but will not *see* Christmas this year.

This is how many will celebrate Christmas. Gifts will be bought and wrapped to place under a Christmas tree. The house will be decorated as in years past with the same lights and same tree in the same place. Cookies will be baked. Parties will be held. School concerts will be attended. Relatives will be entertained or at least endured. They might even make it to church once on Christmas Eve–if for no other reason–so they do not have to lie to their mother when she calls. When Christmas day comes, they will open presents, clean up the mess of wrapping paper, put away all the decorations, and wonder what all the work was for. Because in all that they are *doing*, they will once again miss *seeing* the joy of Christmas.

They will miss the spirit of Christmas because what produces the joy and wonder in our heart is not created by the mere doing of Christmas. True Christmas joy does not just happen in our heart because we pulled out and put up all of the Christmas trappings to adorn our home. For those who believe, the things we do at Christmas happen because true Christmas spirit has already been birthed in our heart. It is the spirit of Christmas that gives meaning to what we do.

So how can we get the spirit of Christmas to reside in our hearts and homes this season? The answer comes in the form of a question: What are you focusing on at Christmas? With all the distractions that will come during the Christmas Season–some good and some perhaps not so good–are you focused on seeing what is truly important for Christmas?

Make no mistake, the world will try to distract you from focusing on the true reason we celebrate Christmas. When it comes to Christmas decorations for your house, have you noticed the store shelves are full of lights, wreaths, and inflatable Santas, but few sell Nativity scenes for your front yard? The reason seems clear: the world wants you to compromise and conform to their secularized version of Christmas. They want you to coexist with how they view Christmas. If you must celebrate, they want you to celebrate Christmas their secularized way. They want you to say "Happy Holidays'" rather than say "Merry Christmas."

And we know why. They are worried saying 'Christmas' will emphasize Christ. The world does not want to acknowledge that Jesus Christ is the only true reason for the Christmas season. But it is the birth of Jesus that we celebrate, not the birth of Santa Claus. In fact, the celebration of Christmas started in the church as the Mass of Christ. The name was simply shortened to Christmas. We are not celebrating the coming of holidays, we are celebrating the coming of Christ.

But, the world wants you to believe that saying "Happy

Holidays" is better; it is the politically correct and more inclusive thing to say. But we are not trying to draw attention to every holiday in December; we are trying to encourage one another about one, particular holiday. Nevertheless, they are worried someone may be offended by you declaring 'Merry Christmas' in their presence. Ironically, by pressuring people to say "Happy Holidays" they prefer to offend the person who believes in Christmas rather than take a chance of offending someone who doesn't even care about Christmas.

Truthfully, they do not want to be reminded of the real purpose of Christmas. The real purpose of Christmas is to recognize that a Savior, Christ the Lord, has come to forgive them of their sin. However, if they recognize a Savior has come, then they will have to acknowledge their sin. And admitting they are a sinner in need of a Savior is something they would rather not do.

But whether we intentionally or innocently slip into the secularized version of Christmas, the result is often the same: we lose our focus and fail to see Jesus at the center of the celebration. So how can we keep our focus when the hustle and bustle of the season press us in and stress us out? How can we see the true spirit of Christmas come alive in our hearts?

Perhaps one could start by asking: what were the people of the original Christmas story looking at on that first Christmas night 2,000 years ago? What were they focused on? The participants of that first Christmas night interrupted their everyday lives to intensely focus on a baby in a manger. What did Mary and Joseph see? What did the shepherds see? What about Herod, the chief priests, and the wise men? What were they looking for? To understand what they saw, to see what they experienced, and to realize how it changed their lives, we must look through their eyes–*Through the Eyes of Christmas*.

CHAPTER 2

MAKE ROOM FOR JESUS

The only way we have to see through the eyes of the participants in the first Christmas story is to look to the Holy Bible. The Word of God accurately, intentionally, and insightfully records the story of each of the Christmas participants.

Only two of the four New Testament gospel writers dealt with the birth of Christ: Matthew and Luke. Matthew tells us about Joseph and the wise men. Luke tells us about Mary, the innkeeper, the manger, the shepherds, and the angels. Both give us a genealogy of Jesus tracing his lineage back to King David, Abraham, and Adam. It is in the Christmas story as related by Matthew and Luke that we gain focus and discover the keys to unlocking the true and lasting spirit of Christmas in our hearts.

Matthew and Luke pull back the celestial curtain of time and reveal the true story of the first Christmas. And while each told the Christmas story from a different perspective, viewed together we see revealed the entire tapestry of God's greatest gift to mankind–a Savior who is Christ the Lord. It is a tapestry that God has been designing for mankind from the foundation of the world.

Matthew writes to the Jews so they will see that Jesus Christ is their Messiah–the fulfillment of the Old Testament prophecies. In the first seventeen verses of Matthew, he gives the genealogy of Jesus through Joseph. He is establishing the royal lineage of Joseph to the House of David and thus to the throne of David. David's throne has been vacant for nearly 600 years, so anyone who would lay claim to David's throne as a rightful king would have to prove his royal lineage back to King David. Matthew establishes Jesus' royal ancestral line back to King David and to the patriarch of all Jews, Abraham. Because the Jews believed the Messiah would be both a descendant of David and Abraham, through this genealogy, Matthew proves the qualification of Jesus as the Messiah and rightful King of Israel. But this belief is not some wished for hope of the ancient Jews, God made covenants with Abraham and King David that the Messiah would come through their seed. (Genesis 17:1-7, 19; 2 Samuel 7:16)

As Matthew traces the genealogy from Abraham to Isaac to Jacob, he takes great care in noting that father begot son, who became a father and begot his son, down all of the generations until he reaches Joseph. There he changes the pattern and specifically states that Joseph was not the father who 'begot' Jesus, but was "the husband of Mary, of whom was born Jesus...." (Matthew

1:16 KJV) Under the law Joseph was, by his marriage to Mary, the legal father of Jesus on Earth. But Matthew and Luke make clear that Joseph was not the biological father of Jesus. Matthew makes this point by using the feminine form of the Greek pronoun that we translate by the words 'of whom,' which could only refer, then, to Mary. Luke uses the angel Gabriel.

This genealogy is an essential prologue to the Christmas story. It not only establishes Jesus as the Christ (meaning the anointed one) and the Messiah, but when overlaid upon the angelic announcement by Gabriel to Mary in Luke chapter 1, we see the virgin birth as prophesied by Isaiah over 700 years before. (Isaiah 7:14) And when Matthew's genealogy of Jesus is overlaid upon the Roman census, it tells us why Joseph and Mary had to travel to Bethlehem, and why Jesus was born in Bethlehem. Joseph and Mary were of the house and in the lineage of King David. Jesus' birth in Bethlehem was the perfect fulfillment of the Jewish prophet Micah's prophecy: it was the location of the birth of the Messiah. (Micah 5:2)

The second Christmas story writer, Luke, wrote to the Gentiles. Luke shows us Mary. He relates the announcement to Mary by the angel Gabriel. He also traces the genealogy of Jesus to establish a royal bloodline through Mary all the way back through King David to Adam (Luke 3:23-38).

Tracing the lineage back to Adam is essential to the Christmas story because it shows why Jesus, the Son of God had to come to Earth. Luke proves Jesus Christ was both the Son of God and the

Son of Man. Sin entered mankind and the world by the disobedience of Adam and Eve. And to cover sin, God's law requires the shedding of innocent blood. (Hebrews 9:22) An animal had to be sacrificed because it was the only innocent substitute available to cover the sin and nakedness of mankind. Sin always brings death as its consequence. And redemption from sin requires an innocent, perfect substitute.

Because Adam was made in the image of God (as all mankind after him), the sacrificial blood of animals would never fully satisfy the requirements for redemption from sin. Although created by God, animals were not made in his image (only mankind was), and therefore animal sacrifice under the Law provided only a temporary covering for sin. Animal sacrifice under the Law had to be repeated annually. "Because it is impossible for the blood of bulls and goats to take away sins." (Hebrews 10:4 NIV) A man made in the image of God, fully divine as God and fully human as a man, would have to sacrifice his sinless blood to offer mankind a permanent redemption for sin. Jesus Christ is that fully God, fully human man who is the only one who qualifies to be the perfect and permanent sacrifice for our sins. (Hebrews 9:28, 10:10)

Luke also gave the historical background as to what happened when Mary and Joseph went to Bethlehem and explains why it happened. He reveals the details of Jesus birth in Bethlehem and the announcement by the angels to shepherds of the Savior's coming. He shows us all of the familiar scenes of the nativity:

the inn, the manger, the shepherds, and the angels. Because Luke gives us these familiar scenes of Christmas, we can start looking for keys to unlocking Christmas spirit there.

Here is how Luke writes the beginning of the most longed-for story the world has ever known:

> "And it came to pass in those days, that there went out a decree from Caesar Augustus, that all the world should be taxed. (And this taxing was first made when Cyrenius was governor of Syria.) And all went to be taxed, every one into his own city. And Joseph also went up from Galilee, out of the city of Nazareth, into Judaea, unto the city of David, which is called Bethlehem; (because he was of the house and lineage of David:) To be taxed with Mary his espoused wife, being great with child. And so it was, that, while they were there, the days were accomplished that she should be delivered. And she brought forth her firstborn son, and wrapped him in swaddling clothes, and laid him in a manger; because there was no room for them in the inn."
>
> (LUKE 2:1-7 KJV)

Luke explains why Jesus was born in a stable and placed in a manger: "...Because there was no room for him in the inn." (Luke 2:7 KJV) In the original Greek–the language used by Luke to write his gospel–Luke uses the word *kataluma* which the King James Bible translated as inn. However, there are two interpretations of the Greek word *kataluma* that can be translated for the inn. One interpretation translates to mean a guest-chamber or guest room of a house; the other interpretation translates to mean a lodging place or a commercial establishment we would recognize as a roadside inn.

Some of the modern Bible translations prefer the first meaning to say there was no guest room available in the house. They speculate Joseph must have still had some shirt-tail relation or possibly old family friends left in Bethlehem, and upon their arrival, Mary and Joseph went to his relation's or some family friend's house.

I suppose it is possible to conjecture that Jesus was born on the ground floor of a two-story Bethlehem house (the ground floor, surrounded by high walls, was the place where the animals were brought in at night; the family lived on the second floor). And I suppose it is possible to believe that Jesus was born on the ground floor with the animals because the guest room on the second floor of the house was already full with Joseph's or some other person's relatives.

But if Jesus had been born on the ground floor of a Bethlehem house and then placed in the feeding trough, with all the relatives around, I think Luke would have made mention of that. And the Christmas story is devoid of mentioning any of Joseph's relatives, even in Bethlehem. It's not to say that Joseph did not have any living relatives; it is just that there is no mention of them in the Christmas story.

Perhaps I'm a bit naïve, but no matter how bad you think your relatives are, making a young girl give birth in an animal's stall and place her firstborn son in a feeding trough when there is a perfectly good guest room above, is just cruel–even for in-laws! So if Joseph had any distant, shirt-tail relation who still lived in Bethlehem, I doubt he and Mary found shelter on the ground floor of their house that first Christmas night.

The second interpretation of the word *kataluma* is an inn or lodging place–the customary thought we have of the roadside inn for travelers coming to Bethlehem. I think it is more likely that Luke meant there was no guest room available in a commercial establishment for travelers. The guest room he referred to could well be the same concept we use today in talking about hotel guests and their guest rooms. The literal meaning of *kataluma* is 'to loose down.' It means the place where travelers would untie (loose) the packages and burdens their animals carried on their journey. It is the place where the travelers loosed their traveling clothes and took off their sandals. It is the place where they broke up their journey. In our modern-day language, it is the place where you unpack and rest for the night.

And behind the inn, tradition places the stable in a small cave, hollowed out of the soft limestone rock. It would have sheltered the animals from the wind and protected them from wild animals. And, it is where the shepherds would have thought to look based upon the angel's sign–find a baby wrapped in swaddling clothes lying in a manger. If Jesus' birthplace had been behind the closed door and walls on the ground floor of a house, I just think the angel would have said so.

All indications point to the fact that Joseph and Mary were strangers to Bethlehem that night. Joseph had likely long since left Bethlehem and established his life and business in the Galilean town of Nazareth. While the Bethlehem inn may have normally been a house for the reception of strangers, that night, not *all* were or could be accepted. Too many other travelers had already taken all available accommodations in Bethlehem. For Mary and Joseph, there was no room in the inn. No reception of strangers; no acceptance.

This seems difficult for us to understand because Mary's predicament would have been evident to all who saw her. Luke makes it clear she was great with child. (Luke 2:5 KJV) That she gave birth later that night means anyone who saw her would have understood her situation; Mary was ready to give birth at any moment. Nevertheless, there was no acceptance. I'm sure Joseph would have pleaded with the innkeeper for mercy under the dire circumstances. But the inn was full. All of the guest rooms were occupied. Perhaps in giving Mary and Joseph use of the stable, the innkeeper did all that he could under the circumstances. Or perhaps, he was just too busy with his other guests to really care.

But did the innkeeper really do all he could that night? He could not overlook Mary's pregnancy, nor her weariness having traveled so far to reach his inn. Did he ask anyone if they would give up their room? Likely he also had a room. But he was apparently not willing to give up his room for Mary and Joseph that night.

Before we judge the innkeeper too harshly, we should remember that it was not only the innkeeper but also the people in the inn who kept Jesus out that night. No guest gave up their accommodations that night for Mary and Joseph. What could they have been thinking?

- "Why should we lose a night's sleep over this couple?"
- "After all, we have already paid for our rooms."
- "Where will we stay if we give up our room to them?"
- "Surely, they can find another place."
- "They should have made better plans."
- "I heard she was pregnant before they got married. This is their problem."
- "It's probably God's judgment on them anyway."

Yes, they likely had plenty of reasons to reject Mary and Joseph that night. But each of their reasons really boiled down to one thing–selfishness. They were more absorbed with their own lives and their needs than in helping the needs of a pregnant woman, ready to give birth, and her husband. And by their own selfishness, or by their own apathy they not only rejected Mary and Joseph but Jesus as well.

And so too, we see the same apathy on the part of so many people during the Christmas season. They seem only concerned about the party shopping and the Christmas shopping, the office parties and dinner parties, the wrapping and decorating, and all of the commotion that often attends Christmas. They are so wrapped up in what they are doing that they miss the gift of the Savior on Christmas day. They seem so preoccupied with the activity surrounding Christmas that they do not realize (or even want to take the time to know) the true purpose of Christmas. So long as they stop by church to put in time on Christmas Eve, they feel they have done their duty to God. To our world, it seems the first coming of Jesus has become just a momentary religious thought amid a secularized monthly holiday.

And if we are not careful, we too will fall victim to the same trap. Christmas comes every year, so why bother. Perhaps we're away from family or maybe have no family. There appears no real reason to celebrate alone. For some, decorating for the Christmas season becomes a job rather than a joy; they'd rather forget the whole thing. But if they do that, they will miss the greatest wonder and awe we can experience in our lives. They will miss the peace and goodwill. They will miss the joy. They will miss the coming of the Savior.

So the people in the inn that first Christmas night did not make room for Jesus. They locked him out of their rooms and shut him out of their hearts. They missed the joyous news that happened right outside their windows. The wondrous birth of their Messiah–the Promised One the Jews had been longing and praying for had finally come. But the people in the inn missed him.

The people inside the inn missed the Messiah's coming. They missed the joy that shepherds saw. They missed the joy–that exceedingly great joy–that the wise men felt in their hearts upon seeing the star and finding the King of Kings, a joy that caused them to worship. They missed the joy experienced by Simeon and Anna–faithful believers who held on to the promise of his coming so fervently that God graciously placed them into the Christmas Story. (Luke 2:25-38) They missed the joy and delight Zachariah and Elizabeth experienced at the birth of their son John, the forerunner of Christ.

The people of Bethlehem missed Jesus that first Christmas because they had no room for him. But we can make room for Jesus at Christmas. We can invite him into our hearts; we can invite him in afresh and anew this season. Let Jesus be a part of everything you do during the Christmas season. Show love to the Marys and Josephs you meet this year. Be accepting. It is the first key to unlock the Christmas Spirit: make room for Jesus in your heart, your home, and for your children.

When Jesus is at the center of your heart, you are well on your way to experiencing the joy that the Christmas season brings. Make room for Jesus this Christmas. Make room in your Christmas decorations to include Jesus. Place a nativity scene on your front lawn to tell your neighbors and all who pass by that Jesus has room in your house this Christmas.

Make room for Jesus in your Christmas shopping: remember those who are less fortunate with your giving. There are many projects from which to choose, from the Angel Tree project to the bell ringers of the Salvation Army. Giving to the least fortunate is making room for Jesus. For Jesus said: "Inasmuch as ye have done it unto one of the least of these my brethren, ye have done it unto me." (Matthew 25:40 KJV)

Make room for Jesus in your celebrating. Don't let the temporal materialism of the masses around you (or the material temptations of merchants in front of you) crowd Jesus out of your heart. Don't focus on what you want or what you get (or didn't get). Focus instead on the joy of your giving. Help others, especially the children, see that the joy of Christmas is spread abroad by what we give others, not by what we receive. Remember, God loves a cheerful giver. (2 Corinthians 9:7 NIV)

Make room for Jesus on Christmas Day. Before you rush to open the brightly wrapped packages under the tree, open his Word. Read his story and see the true meaning of this day come to life in your home. Do this first and you will see the joy of Christmas glow brightly in your life this Christmas season.

CHAPTER 3

THIS MUST BE THE PLACE

Have you ever wondered why God chose Bethlehem to be the place where Jesus would come into our world? Why should he be born in Bethlehem? And if it is going to be Bethlehem, how do you get Mary and Joseph there? After all, each of them lives in Nazareth, about 90 miles to the north.

The simple and historical reason Mary and Joseph travel to Bethlehem is that they were commanded to by a Roman census decree. The Roman Caesar whose army occupied and controlled all of Israel – in fact controlled all of the then known world – decided it was time again to register and take a census of all of the adult males in the Roman Empire. Of the three known censuses taken by Caesar Augustus, this was likely the one decreed in 8 BC, because it coincides with the first time Cyrenius was governor of Syria (he actually ruled as the administrator of Syria twice). Luke took special care to date the birth of Jesus to known rulers, like Caesar Augustus and Cyrenius, of whom historical records would be written and verifiable. And since Caesar Augustus lacked modern computing and communication methods, the census was probably decreed in 8 BC and then organized, administered and conducted over several years until its completion.

This then puts Jesus birth between 6 and 4 BC, right when Cyrenius was governor. For all the advances in technology and time, the slow-moving bureaucracy–whether ancient Roman or modern day–apparently has not changed.

The purpose of the Roman census was not only to see who was able to work and thus pay tax, but also who could be conscripted to serve in the Roman army. And while Jews were not required to serve in the Roman army, they could not escape taxation.

Because Judea was still a kingdom (albeit an occupied one) and not a province of Rome, the Romans permitted the census to be taken in accordance with the Jewish custom. The Jews conducted a census registration not by the city of residence, but by the city of ancestral birth.

Why the city of birth? Because that is where the original documents would have been kept if any such records existed. But more likely, it was where all of the people who knew you lived. They would know who you were and could attest to who your parents were, and grandparents, aunts, uncles, and the rest of your relatives. They would know what street you grew up on, what house you lived in, what your occupation was, and all of the other relevant and likely gossiping, non-relevance that follows our lives. In a world where the written word was rare, this kind of oral history was indispensable to prove who you were and where you came from. And proving your pure ancestral lineage back to the Jewish patriarchs, Abraham, Isaac, and Jacob was essential for the Jews.

So the world of Bethlehem that first Christmas night was focused on the Roman registration. It was, quite literally, the talk of the town. Think of it: every Jew who was ever born in Bethlehem, whose family lineage was traced to that town through King David, had to return to Bethlehem.

The normal population swelled to overwhelm the tiny hamlet. People were hustling and bustling about, trying to find accommodations for the night. They were visiting with relatives and long-lost friends who had reunited in their hometown. Yes, they were busy with the cares of life and not the least bit concerned about the arrival of a very pregnant Jewish girl and her husband. To the world of Bethlehem, Mary and Joseph were just another couple of people in town for the night.

And while in one respect Mary and Joseph's travel to Bethlehem fulfilled their duty to a Roman census, from God's perspective it was the fulfillment of prophecy. Using a Roman census to bring Mary and Joseph to Bethlehem may seem unconventional to us, but we should remember that God can, and often, will use any means he deems necessary to accomplish his purpose–whether improbable or even impossible. If God can make the wrath of man to praise him (Psalms 76:10), it is no difficult task for God to put a census decree into the mind of the Roman Caesar Augustus. So Caesar Augustus may have thought it was time to register and take a census of all of the adult males in the Roman Empire, but Luke highlights God's providential hand in the story.

Luke opens the Christmas story with the words: *"And it came to pass."* (Luke 2:1 KJV) That phrase 'and it came to pass' is more than just an introductory clause in scripture. Those seemingly minor transitional words, upon closer examination, reveal that God was and really is in control.

The word "pass" in the Greek means *to cause to* be or to generate. In other words there is a divine actor behind the scenes causing the events to come into being. The events do not occur by happenstance in the ordinary course of time; God is ordering their occurence to happen at this particular time. Any time you read 'and it came to pass' in your Bible, you should interpret that phrase to mean in God's perfect time. In this occurrence, it means in God's perfect time, Christ was sent to the world.

In Galatians, Apostle Paul reminds us, "But when the fullness of the time was come, God sent forth his Son, made of a woman, made under the law, [t]o redeem them that were under the law, that we might receive the adoption of sons." (Galatians 4:4–5 KJV) Paul is pointing out that God uses our time to fulfill his plans. The key is the fullness of God's perfect timing. Things come to pass in our lives because God says it is now time for them to be. His plan, his purpose brings these things to pass. It is God's fullness of time that has come to pass that first Christmas night in Bethlehem.

It was not happenstance or coincidence that caused Jesus to be born at that moment in history. Out of his infinite, everlasting love, God gave Jesus to the world. He said so. "For God so loved the world that he gave his only begotten Son, that whosoever believeth in him should not perish, but have everlasting life." (John 3:16 KJV) God gave this great gift of himself not to condemn the world, but that the world through Jesus might be saved. (John 3:17) God's gifts are not by chance, and the timing of their giving is not by coincidence. Just as you give thought and select the Christmas gifts you are going to give, so too did God select and perfectly time the giving of himself manifested to us in God the Son, his perfect gift of salvation to all men.

But, why then? What was so special about the world over 2,000 years ago? For one thing, the Roman Empire stretched across the known geography of the world. Rome had built highways to every corner of its empire, connecting the furthest part with every other part. All roads truly led to Rome. There was one common language known to all: not Latin, but Greek. After Alexander the Great, Greek had become the common language of not only commerce and diplomacy but of the common man in the street as well. It became a common language of communication between cultures. And Caesar Augustus had achieved forty-four years of peace (or at least peaceful occupation from a Roman point of view). So Christ came when the gospel could be spread quickly, effectively, and efficiently throughout the entire world.

But there is a more telling reason: God's Word. The interpretation by the Old Testament prophet Daniel of King Nebuchadnezzar's great image dream foretold of the rise of a fourth kingdom as strong as iron. (Daniel 2:40) That kingdom is the Roman Empire which began about 67 BC and conquered the then known world, growing beyond the size of any of the kingdoms preceding it. Daniel foretold of a stone cut out of a mountain without hands representing the Messiah who will smite the image at its feet of iron and clay and brake them to pieces. Thereafter shall the God of heaven set up a kingdom which shall never be destroyed, it will destroy all other kingdoms and shall stand forever. (Daniel 2:44) So to fulfill Daniel's prophecy, Jesus the Messiah, could not come until after the establishment and world domination of the fourth kingdom, the Roman Empire.

Moreover, God spoke through his prophet Malachi, saying: "BEHOLD, I will send my messenger, and he shall prepare the way before me: and the Lord, whom ye seek, shall suddenly come to his temple, even the messenger of the covenant, whom ye delight in: behold, he shall come, saith the LORD of hosts." (Malachi 3:1 KJV) The Temple in Jerusalem was destroyed by the Romans in AD 70 and has never been rebuilt, not even to this day nearly 2,000 years later. So for Jesus the Messiah to fulfill

God's prophetic Word through Malachi, for Jesus to enter the Temple and baffle the religious leaders at age twelve, for Jesus to overturn the money changers' tables in the Temple at age thirty-three, there had to be a Temple for Jesus to come to. And Jesus had to come to the Temple when the fourth kingdom, the Roman Empire ruled the world. So, Jesus had to come at that precise moment in history.

But all our reasoning and speculation matters little, for God decided it was time. And that is enough. What is more he had already decided the place. Eight hundred years before Jesus' coming, the prophet Micah foretold: "But thou, Bethlehem Ephratah, though thou be little among the thousands of Judah, yet out of thee shall he come forth unto me that is to be ruler in Israel; whose goings forth have been from of old, from everlasting." (Micah 5:2 KJV)

And notice that while God chose Bethlehem to be the birthplace, Micah reminded us that this future ruler of Israel has existed from old, from everlasting. In other words, Jesus, the Son of God wasn't born then. He has always existed. He exists from everlasting. The Son of God is eternal God with no beginning and no end. Bethlehem wasn't the beginning of the Son of God; it was the place where the eternal, ever-existent, divine God took on human flesh manifested to us as Jesus the Son of God, so he could be our Savior. (Philippians 2:5–8)

The place the Messiah would be born was no secret. Apparently, everyone (except Herod) knew it. The chief priests and scribes knew it when they told Herod during the wise men's visit to Jerusalem. The people all knew it when they argued about Jesus being the Christ in John 7:42. (By that time, Christ had grown up in Nazareth and the people disputed that Jesus was the Messiah because he wasn't from Bethlehem...or so they thought.) Yet, for all their supposed knowledge of where Messiah would be born, they still missed his coming.

And why did God choose Bethlehem? There was nothing special about this little hamlet, just seven miles or so south of Jerusalem. But there is one point of significance. Bethlehem–the city of King David's birth, the direct ancestor of Joseph (and of Mary)–was called the House of Bread. It is what the word "Bethlehem" means.

It makes sense when you understand the geography. Bethlehem was surrounded by grain fields, and the town's bakeries supplied bread to Jerusalem. It makes sense that Jesus, who declared himself to be the Bread of Life in John 6:35, was born in the town known as the House of Bread. He becomes a type of the Old Testament manna: the provision of everlasting, life-sustaining bread to his chosen people Israel, and by personal acceptance to all people. I believe manna–which by definition meant "What is it?"–tasted like whatever you wanted it to taste like. And Jesus came as the Bread of Life in the House of Bread so that we would know he is here to sustain us. He is here for whatever we need.

So although great with child, Mary and Joseph go to Bethlehem. Perhaps in their minds, the trip to Bethlehem was only to fulfill the law of Rome. But in God's perfect time, God used it to fulfill his word to his people. And let's not forget, going to Bethlehem is no small task for a pregnant woman–being great with child–traveling ninety miles from Nazareth which is three days by donkey! While there is no logical reason why such a pregnant woman would wish to travel so far under such difficult conditions, there is no mention in the Christmas story of resistance or doubt on the part of Mary. Perhaps that is really why she is called a saint!

It is not always easy or convenient doing God's will. It may not even be comfortable to serve God in your circumstances. But the glorious outcome of obedience is always far greater than the discomfort and inconvenience we may endure in the "come to pass" parts of our lives.

And so it was accomplished. Jesus the Bread of Life is born in the House of Bread. He is placed in a manger; a feeding trough, because he is the bread by which we receive life. Jesus was born in a stable because the inn had no room for him. I can only imagine that Joseph heard the commotion outside the stable as the shepherds burst in saying to each other: "Look there is the baby in the manger. This must be the place!"

But not everyone who is searching for the place to find Christmas will be successful. There are those who will search in vain for the real meaning of Christmas. Without a clear direction of where to find the true spirit of Christmas, they resort to the only form of Christmas they know. They buy into the secularized version of Christmas, only to find that in all their Christmas *doing*, they are once again deprived of *seeing* Christmas spirit in their heart. True Christmas spirit cannot be found in a secular setting that only honors the world's substitutes.

Some search for Christmas spirit with the wrong motives. Like Herod, they consult their religious leaders to find out where Jesus, this new King of the Jews, is to be born. But they lack the understanding to know what their counselors have told them. They search in the wrong places to find the Christ child. He is not in the shopping or in Santa. He isn't in the Christmas TV specials or on the umpteenth viewing of *It's a Wonderful Life*. Jesus isn't born in the malls or office parties. And so they miss the coming of Jesus; they miss him just like the people of Bethlehem that first Christmas night, even though he is right outside their rooms, resting comfortably in a lowly manger.

The place for Christmas in your heart must be intentionally made. You need to make a special place for Christmas in your home. Whether around traditional Christmas decorations, or just around a simple nativity, there should be a place where you can go and sit and see Christmas with your eyes. It should be a place that others will recognize as dedicated to Christmas in your home.

God felt the place of Jesus birth so important, that he had Micah prophesy about it hundreds of years before Jesus came to Earth. It was so important that God commanded a special star to move at his command and shine directly over where Jesus was. Without that star, the wise men would have never found Jesus. And therein lies another key to the Christmas spirit–make a place in your heart and home for Christmas to be seen: by you and by all who come to visit you. When you do it right, others will, like the shepherds, exclaim: "This must be the place where the spirit of Christmas is!"

CHAPTER 4

SURRENDERED SERVICE

Even little girls have big dreams. Mary was no different. I am sure she daydreamed about her life with Joseph, her betrothed. With all of his carpentry skills, she had to wonder what the house would look like...and the kitchen...and the bedroom. What was Joseph building?

I am sure she envisioned the perfect Jewish household. She and Joseph would live in Nazareth, a town in the hill country on the southwest side of the Sea of Galilee. He would work at his carpentry trade, maybe have a shop in the middle of town. He would come home for lunch each day. She would care for the house and there would be children. They would attend synagogue each Sabbath, and they would all serve God.

Mary's thoughts were not only of Joseph. She had a deep understanding of God. Mary was a magnifier–a worshipper if you will. *To magnify* means *to enlarge; to make great.* To Mary, her worship magnified God. In her worship, she magnified God to make him greater, larger in her everyday life. She knew God as mighty, with a strong arm, and able to do great things. She knew God as holy and she reverenced his very name. Perhaps, because Mary was a magnifier, a worshiper, and a faithful follower, God chose her to be the virgin vessel through whom the salvation of Israel and salvation of the world would come. Here is how Luke records this revelation to Mary, and therein how we can see through Mary's eyes that first Christmas:

> *"And in the sixth month the angel Gabriel was sent from God unto a city of Galilee, named Nazareth, [t]o a virgin espoused to a man whose name was Joseph, of the house of David; and the virgin's name was Mary.*
>
> *And the angel came in unto her, and said, Hail, thou that art highly favored, the Lord is with thee: blessed art thou among women. And when she saw him, she was troubled at his saying, and cast in her mind what manner of salutation this should be. And the angel said unto her, Fear not, Mary: for thou hast found favour with God. And, behold, thou shalt conceive in thy womb, and bring forth a son, and shalt call his name JESUS. He shall be great, and shall be called the Son of the Highest: and the Lord God shall give unto him the throne of his father David: And he shall reign over the house of Jacob forever; and of his kingdom there shall be no end. Then said Mary*

unto the angel, [h]ow shall this be, seeing I know not a man? And the angel answered and said unto her, The Holy Ghost shall come upon thee, and the power of the Highest shall overshadow thee: therefore also that holy thing which shall be born of thee shall be called the Son of God. And, behold, thy cousin Elisabeth, she hath also conceived a son in her old age: and this is the sixth month with her, who was called barren. For with God nothing shall be impossible. And Mary said, Behold the handmaid of the Lord; be it unto me according to thy word. And the angel departed from her."

(LUKE 1:26–38 KJV)

There, in one supernatural moment, Mary's life changed forever. She is interrupted in her day-dreaming by the angel Gabriel's greeting: "You are highly favored by God, the Lord is with thee."

God's favor is simply the exercise of his grace. He extends grace to us. Grace means unmerited, undeserved, unrequested favor. Grace cannot be earned, and it comes to us without any merit that we deserve it. Grace comes not because we ask for it but it comes because our Heavenly Father loves to abundantly pour it out upon us. Nothing we can do, no good deed, no extravagant kindness can ever impress God. In fact, compared to the purest perfection of his holiness, all of our best righteous acts are nothing but filthy rags in his sight. (Isaiah 64:6) So God's grace steps in to pour out His favor upon us.

While God's love pours out favor to us, it is what we do with that favor that is vitally important and makes a difference in our lives. If we use God's grace selfishly (ignoring God's gracious gift) or as a license to live in sin, we misappropriate God's favor in our lives. Unfortunately, some will think God's outpouring of favor was of their own making and arrogantly use it to increase themselves in the eyes of others. In Matthew chapter 6, Jesus pointed out these type of individuals. They squandered God's favor in their life by outward shows of self-righteous piety. They claimed God's blessings as their own doing. Jesus said those individuals have their reward. (Matthew 6:2)

Mary remained humble and godly in her life as God poured out his favor upon her. And Mary was highly favored by God, so much so that God's very presence attended his outpouring of grace upon her.

Yet, the angel's greeting perplexed Mary because she did not see herself as highly favored. At that moment, Mary did not think herself "blessed among all women." She was the poorest of the poor. She viewed herself as a lowly handmaiden. She felt unworthy of the greeting.

But in Gabriel's greeting, we see what God thought of her. She was the recipient of divine grace–unmerited favor that brought God's presence, plan, and purpose into her life. It is just a side note, but it is often far more important to realize what God thinks of us than it is to dwell upon what we think of ourselves. God gives us his grace for a divine reason.

But this outpouring of grace and presence came at a great cost. Mary must give up all that she had planned to accept something she had never planned for–something that wasn't even humanly possible. It is not humanly possible for a virgin to give birth, but as the angel Gabriel points out, nothing is impossible with God. Was she willing to set aside her dreams, her plans, her ambitions, and submit to the plans and purposes that God had for her life?

This is a very difficult question to answer. This is not a "let me get back to you on this" kind of moment. Mary's decision is needed now. But God is not asking her to simply change her plans. This is a never-happened-in-the-history-of-the-world kind of change! Virgin birth? How do you explain that to your mother? What do you tell Joseph? After all, she was betrothed to Joseph, and in the eyes of the synagogue and society, she was legally married to him.

I can imagine Mary's thoughts at that moment. Suddenly, the reality of what God was asking of her sunk in. How am I going to explain this to Joseph? What will he say? How will he react? What about my family...and friends? She had to know the consequences if Joseph did not believe her. He would divorce her, she would lose the man she loved, and if her family rejected her too, she would have to raise this child alone. She was being asked to bear reproach and ridicule for the rest of her life, even though she was completely pure and innocent of any wrong-doing. Unfortunately, the world never understands the Divine, much less the deep things of God.

And while all these thoughts are swirling in her head and her heart is pounding so hard in her chest that she is fighting just to breathe, she asks this angelic visitor one question: "How shall this be, seeing I know not a man?" It is almost as if she asks the question so she has time to think, time to catch her breath, time to calm her heart. But it is her question that allows God to enter the situation and speak peace. Gabriel's answer brings all of the swirling thoughts to perfect rest.

To the question of how, Gabriel simply answers: God, the Holy Spirit. That's the answer. That's always the answer. That is the answer that has always been and will always be. That's all the answer we need to the perplexing problems we face throughout the year. When we allow his perfect peace to take charge of the affairs of our life, we will supplant our preoccupations with his preeminence. We will release the cares of our lives–the preoc-cupations we have crafted into so-called priorities–and replace them with the peace that only God can offer.

For Mary, the overshadowing of the Holy Spirit, his complete covering, his presence, and his guidance is all she will need to accept God's plan and purpose in her life. It is all she will need to face Joseph, her relatives, and friends. His peace is all she will need to face their reactions or decisions over which she has no control. He is all she will need to be the prophesied virgin who will conceive and bring forth the Savior who is Christ the Lord.

But Gabriel offers her more. As proof of his statement "with God nothing shall be impossible," Gabriel informs her that Mary's aged cousin Elizabeth, the one they call barren, is in the sixth month of her pregnancy. It wasn't just to prove that God could answer Zachariah's and Elizabeth's prayer for a child, now that they were old and past childbearing. God had released barrenness in the lives of so many women, like Sarah, Rebekah, Rachel, and even a Shunammite woman–old and young alike. But in Elizabeth's case it was a miracle with divine purpose, and God wanted Mary to know that she too could experience a divinely purposed miracle in her life, because nothing is impossible with God.

Upon hearing the angel's answer, Mary utters an incredible, yet now fully understandable, statement. She tells Gabriel: "Behold the handmaid of the Lord; be it unto me according to thy word." (Luke 1:38 KJV) What a declaration of faith in God!

To understand her declaration of faith, we need only look at two words of her statement: "Behold" and "handmaid." For in the word "Behold", we see total surrender and complete acceptance. In that instant, she fully surrendered all of her dreams, plans, and ambitions to the revelation of God's will for her life. Her declaration "Behold" said: *Look. The girl you greeted is no more; I have accepted, surrendered to, and have been changed by God's word.*

In uttering "Behold," Mary emptied herself of everything–who she thought she was and who she thought she wanted to be. She released all that her human efforts could attain and all that she could receive in this world. Gone were her desires; her plans no longer mattered. She surrendered all to fulfill the calling that God had placed upon her life. And in this surrender, she received back all that she had dreamed of as a little girl. She would still be a mother and wife, but now, she was the mother of the Savior of the world and her purpose had divine perspective. She would be blessed among all women because she was willing to be used by God to fulfill his plan of redemption for the world.

We often sing all of the verses and chorus of that sacred hymn "I Surrender All," somehow praying that God will sense the sincerity we are trying to muster with our voice. Mary said it all in one word: *behold*. And, in that same word, she not only surrendered all but equally and fully accepted all. She accepted all of God's plans and purpose for her life–whatever the cost.

All of that makes sense when combined with the second word in her statement: *handmaid*. In the Greek, she used the term for a female servant. In effect, she was saying to God: *I am no longer a free person in control of my life. I choose to be and now belong to the Lord; I am his servant. His way is now my way. His plan is now my plan. His purpose is now my purpose.*

The word "handmaid" means one whose essential and necessary purpose is to serve another. But she declares this servanthood with overwhelming JOY. "Be it unto me" is not a statement of resignation; it is a victorious shout of rejoicing. She is the one of whom Isaiah prophesied: "Therefore the Lord himself shall give you a sign; Behold, a virgin shall conceive, and bear a son, and shall call his name Immanuel." (Isaiah 7:14 KJV) She is the one who will bring Messiah to her people! Mary will be the mother that gets to hug, hold, and kiss the face of God. And that shows us what she was looking at that Christmas: Mary sees Christmas through the eyes of surrendered service.

Can you handle God's changes in your life with humility and surrendered service? The steps of a righteous man are ordered of the Lord, and so, I believe, are the stops as well. We will not be asked to make the kind of sacrifice Mary had to endure, but on the smaller stages of our lives, can we tell God, "I am your servant this Christmas?"

What will be your prayer to God this Christmas? To follow in Mary's footsteps, you have to be willing to pray: "God, I'll go where you want me to go. I'll serve where you want me to serve. I am willing to be used by you however you want. This Christmas my gift to you is me."

Adopting the humble attitude of a servant this Christmas is another key to unlocking the spirit of Christmas in your heart. Giving of yourself, a gift of your time to others is the rarest, most precious, and most extravagant gift you can give another. Serving others is how the spirit of Christmas can rise up in your heart. True and lasting joy is found in serving others. Each time you serve others, you rekindle the joy and perpetuate the spirit of Christmas in your life. When so much of the secular focus is on ourselves–what we want and what we get–it will be a drastic and refreshing change to intentionally place the focus on serving others. When it comes to obtaining the joy that fosters the spirit of Christmas, it is always better to say: "God, I am at your service."

CHAPTER 5

JUST OBEDIENCE

Joseph's Christmas story is quite different from Mary's story, but completely in keeping with why God chose him to be the legal guardian and earthly father to Jesus. Matthew records his story beginning in Matthew 1:18.

"Now the birth of Jesus Christ was on this wise: When as his mother Mary was espoused to Joseph before they came together, she was found with child of the Holy Ghost. Then Joseph her husband, being a just man, and not willing to make her a public example, was minded to put her away privily.

But while he thought on these things, behold, the angel of the Lord appeared unto him in a dream, saying, Joseph, thou son of David, fear not to take unto thee Mary thy wife: for that which is conceived in her is of the Holy Ghost.

And she shall bring forth a son, and thou shalt call his name JESUS: for he shall save his people from their sins.

Now all this was done, that it might be fulfilled which was spoken of the Lord by the prophet, saying, Behold, a virgin shall be with child, and shall bring forth a son, and they shall call his name Emmanuel, which being interpreted is, God with us.

Then Joseph being raised from sleep did as the angel of the Lord had bidden him, and took unto him his wife: And knew her not till she had brought forth her firstborn son: and he called his name JESUS."

(MATTHEW 1:18–25 KJV)

Like Mary, Joseph had plans and dreams about how his life with Mary would be. And like Mary, Joseph was asked by God to change all of his dreams and aspirations and yield to the plan of God. But I imagine–as only a man possibly can–that Joseph's thoughts both frustrated and perplexed him all at the same time.

His heart was broken. His dreams and hopes had been shattered by the news that Mary was with child. How could this have happened? How could Mary do this to me? I thought she loved me. She accepted the betrothal and now this? Who could do such a thing? All he knew was, it was not his doing. But if this news got any further, under the Law of Moses, Mary could be put to death. By the existence of the betrothal they were, in the eyes of the law, married. Matthew makes this point clear in the text by identifying Mary as "espoused to Joseph" and Joseph as "her husband." (Matthew 1:18-19) In the simple realities that he faced, I believe the faith he knew in his head told him to do the only thing his heart could handle. He would put her away privately by divorce, rather than expose her to public disgrace and probable death.

It is reasonable to conclude that Joseph felt betrayed. But to fully understand his predicament, you need to understand what betrothal meant. In Joseph's day, marriage was made up of two separate events, formalized by a written contract: the betrothal period and the marriage or wedding. And while the marriage was not consummated until after the wedding, the couple was considered married as husband and wife after the betrothal period was entered. So to call off or end the marriage after the betrothal period started required a bill of divorcement.

The betrothal would be formalized by legally binding Writings of Betrothal which set forth: (a) the amount to be paid to the bride's father; (b) the mutual promises of the bride and groom; and (c) all of the other terms of the marriage (for example, where they would live). In this first century agricultural society, the bride's father was typically paid to compensate him for the loss of a daughter and the labor, contribution, and value she had brought to his household. And because the bride was typically joining her husband's father's household (remember that extended families often lived under one roof), the duties she would perform there would be spelled out in the Writings of Betrothal.

The Marriage or wedding was not so much a ceremony as it was a procession, followed by a feast. It involved the groom, getting together with all of his friends and parading over to the bride's house, where she and all of her bridesmaids were waiting. They would then all go back to the groom's house (typically the father's house) and there have a simple ceremony and feast. Remember the parable of the wise and foolish virgins that Jesus told in Matthew 25? He described this customary practice of the bridegroom coming to get his bride and returning to his house for the marriage or wedding feast.

Depending on their age, the young men of Joseph's time could choose their bride and if they did so, would inform their family. The bride's family would be contacted and, if the bride freely and willingly consented to the betrothal and marriage, then the families would work out the details. Those details could then be taken to the religious authorities, like the rabbi of the synagogue, who would draw up the Writings of Betrothal contract.

The acceptance of the Writings was completed at a simple ceremony between the families. The bride and groom would sit down and the Writings of Betrothal would be read aloud in front of the bride. This was her last chance to express her acceptance or rejection of the prospective engagement and marriage to the groom.

Because a Writing of Betrothal was a legally binding

contract, the bride must consent of her own free will in order for the Writing of Betrothal to be contractually enforceable. If she accepted, she would take her cup and drink. The groom would place a ring on the bride's finger (or if he could not afford a ring, give the bride some other token). The Writings of Betrothal would thus be formalized and in the eyes of Jewish law, family, and synagogue, they were husband and wife. The betrothal period thus began; typically nine months to a year for the very obvious reason.

While we are not told how Writings of Betrothal may have happened between Mary and Joseph, we do know that Mary was betrothed to Joseph. She would have been treated as if she were actually married to Joseph. So to be found with child before the marriage ceremony was adultery in the eyes of the community and grounds for divorce. But more than that, she could be put to death for committing adultery under the Law of Moses. (Leviticus 20:10)

Into this turmoil, God gently speaks words of encouragement and direction to Joseph. God did not send an angel to speak to an awake, alert, and conscious Joseph. He spoke into Joseph's dreams. God spoke into Joseph's broken dreams so that Joseph could see God as the restorer of broken dreams. God's redemptive plan is not just about salvation. It is also about restoration. It is about repairing our broken dreams, restoring our stolen dreams, and giving us the desires of our heart as we delight in him. (Psalms 37:4)

For Joseph, God sent angelic comfort to his broken heart. And, we can get a clue as to Joseph's emotional state from the very first words the angel speaks: "Do not be afraid to take Mary home as your wife because what is conceived in her is from the Holy Spirit." (Matthew 1:20 NIV)

"Fear not" are often the first words we hear from angelic beings in Scripture. I believe it is not just because their presence is so alarming to us that we are paralyzed in fright but more importantly, it is only when fear is removed from the situation that our faith has the chance to flourish. It is because the opponent of faith is not doubt; it is fear. Since angels are the messengers of God and are sent to us for a specific and very important purpose, God really does need us to trust him in that moment. And that trust requires faith, not fear.

But Joseph is also just and devout. What will others in the synagogue think if he marries Mary after she is found with child? They will whisper that his devotion to God was mere lip service; he says one thing but acts just like the rest of us. If Joseph took Mary to be his wife now, how could he face his friends, his family, and his community? What about his carpentry business? Will he lose customers because they think he is a hypocrite?

Joseph is faced with a dilemma. Being devout means that he is righteous in observing divine laws. He is upright in keeping God's commands. His way of thinking, feeling, and acting is wholly conformed to the will of God.

We know this not only because of the words Matthew uses to

describe Joseph but also because of one other reference we have of Joseph in the Bible–the trip to Jerusalem when Jesus is twelve. The Bible tells us it was Joseph and Mary's custom to go up to Jerusalem each year at Passover. They were in that observance devout–not so much in keeping an eye on where their 12-year-old son had gotten off to. You'll remember that they lost track of him (Jesus was actually in the Temple astounding the Doctors of the Law), and it took them three days to find him.

So a man who is devoted to God, who righteously and consistently follows God's commands finds out his beloved fiancé is with child. He loves Mary and wants to show compassion. The Law of Moses gave him two options: bring her before the Synagogue and have her stoned to death or put her away privately by a bill of divorce. The first option was a real threat. Remember the woman brought to Jesus, caught in the act of adultery? (John 8:3-11) The scribes and Pharisees were ready to stone that woman to death. The second option involved only 2 witnesses and his statement of divorce.

But which option should he choose? Revenge for the embarrassment and violation of his honor might choose the first option. But as a righteous and devout Jew, Joseph is also likely aware of Psalms 112:4-5 which directs an upright man to be gracious, full of compassion, while being righteous. So Joseph's thinking is leaning towards the bill of divorcement. But he doesn't want to lose Mary forever either. Joseph has come to a fork in the road and both sides seem right. Which way should he choose? Here is where God enters the situation to give comfort and direction.

Joseph receives the same answer that Mary got to her question: do not be afraid; this is a God-thing. God steps into Joseph's story to tell him that the plans he is directing in Joseph's life contain divine possibilities. Carrying out the plan will be difficult and probably painful. Yes, there may be whispers, and perhaps outright accusations. But a decision to follow God's plan is empowered with God's ordained purpose. Joseph is to be the legal guardian and earthly father to the Savior of the world.

And because Joseph was both a devout Jew and a righteous man (i.e., in right standing before God), God spoke to him in a way that Joseph would understand. God reminded him of Isaiah's prophecy in Isaiah 7:14: "Behold, a virgin shall be with child and shall bring forth a son, and they shall call his name Emmanuel, which, being interpreted is God with us." (Matthew 1:23 KJV) God wanted Joseph to know he was living in the fulfillment of God's word to his people. Mary's pregnancy was not a mistake; it was a miracle of God's fulfilling prophecy. Mary, his Mary, was the one God had chosen to be the virgin with child.

And the God-chosen name Immanuel, who was to be born of Mary, did not just mean "God was now with us" in physical presence, but it also and most importantly meant that because a Savior had come, God was **with** us and no longer **against** us! Because Immanuel has come, God is now on our side.

In that moment, everything that had happened now made

perfect sense. The confusing scriptures he had heard read at synagogue are now clear. He was being asked to be part of the plan for the salvation of the world.

What fascinates me most about Joseph's role in the Christmas story is that Joseph is never recorded in sacred scripture as saying anything; not one word. He is revealed to us as a man of deep thought, conviction, and faith. He is a man who is just and devout. His relationship with God is right. His thoughts tell us he is compassionate. But his actions demonstrate he is also a man who obeys immediately. Joseph trusts God. Joseph believes God. So, Joseph proved his faith by what he did, not what he said.

Rising from his sleep, Joseph takes decisive action: he goes to Mary, brings her to his house, and takes her to be his wife. All the fear that he had held in his heart melted away at the thought of participating in the fulfillment of God's prophetic Word.

All of this shows us what Joseph was looking at that Christmas. Joseph saw Christmas through the eyes of obedience, just obedience. And notice, obedience is a perfect companion to the surrendered service of a humble servant. One fully understands the other. Each completes the other. Each complements the other. Mary and Joseph are God's perfect choices for each other.

But even with a perfect helpmate, life will throw difficulties in our path. How do we face the challenges that come our way, especially during Christmas? How do we respond when unwarranted ridicule and criticism comes our way–especially from our family? Can we be still and know he is God? Can we trust his way, even if we cannot see his path? Are we obedient enough to walk by faith, and not by sight? Accepting God's plans in faithful obedience, even when we don't fully understand, will let us focus intently on the true meaning of the Christ Child–Immanuel, God with us.

Obedience to God's Word is another key that unlocks the spirit of Christmas in our heart. It is knowing the true meaning of the Christmas story so well that we can see opportunities to put the message of Christmas to work in our lives and in the lives of those around us. And it is not just the knowing when it comes to obedience; it is the doing through which we can show others the way to the true spirit of Christmas. Can others see the Christ of Christmas in you?

CHAPTER 6

SHARING JESUS WITH OTHERS

The next key to unlock the Christmas Spirit in your heart and home this Christmas season is seen in the story of the shepherds. God chose the lowliest in status to announce the greatest salvation. Luke Chapter 2 relates to us this inspiring segment of the Christmas story.

"And there were in the same country shepherds abiding in the field, keeping watch over their flock by night. And, lo, the angel of the Lord came upon them, and the glory of the Lord shone round about them: and they were sore afraid. And the angel said unto them, 'Fear not: for, behold, I bring you good tidings of great joy, which shall be to all people. For unto you is born this day in the city of David a Saviour, which is Christ the Lord. And this shall be a sign unto you; Ye shall find the babe wrapped in swaddling clothes, lying

in a manger.' And suddenly there was with the angel a multitude of the heavenly host praising God and saying, 'Glory to God in the highest, and on earth peace, good will toward men.' And it came to pass, as the angels were gone away from them into heaven, the shepherds said one to another, 'Let us now go even unto Bethlehem, and see this thing which is come to pass, which the Lord hath made known unto us.' And they came with haste, and found Mary, and Joseph, and the babe lying in a manger. And when they had seen it, they made known abroad the saying which was told them concerning this child. And all they that heard it wondered at those things which were told them by the shepherds."

(Luke 2:8–18 KJV)

Why shepherds? To answer that question we need to know more about who they were and why they were "abiding in the field, keeping watch over their flock by night." Shepherds were of the lowliest estate in Israel. They were typically the most unskilled, uneducated, unambitious people in the society. If you had no other skills, no other talents, no other calling, *you* could be a shepherd! They were common and ordinary, doing the simplest of tasks–watching sheep. But we know that God does not exclude people based on their ethnic or socio-economic status. (Acts 10:34) It doesn't matter what you do for a living or how much you make, God loves you and wants you to know the miraculous incarnation of the Son of God, Jesus.

And while we celebrate Christmas in December, Bible theologians tell us that it was likely during the spring of the year that Jewish shepherds would be found out in the fields at night. This is the time of year when most of the lambs are born.

What were the shepherds doing? They were abiding. In the original, it means literally to camp-out. This is not a minor point. Jesus emphasized it this way: "If ye abide in me and my words abide in you, ye shall ask what ye will and it shall be done unto you." (John 15:7 KJV) These are powerful words of promise from the one who can do what he said. The only condition to the fulfillment of this promise is our obedience to abide, to camp-out, to take up residence in Christ and let his words live in us. Is it possible that these lowly shepherds were also abiding in the Word? Could they have been chosen because they were willing to believe that the promise of the Savior had come?

But why announce the world's greatest news to shepherds? Why not tell the chief priests and scribes? Simply stated: they were not ready to receive the glad tidings of great joy. Oh, they knew where the Christ would be born. They even told Herod (Matthew 2:4–5). But they did not want to believe their own words. Their actions towards Jesus and his ministry revealed that they were more interested in maintaining the religious status quo than in finding their Messiah and Savior.

What about the Pharisees or Sadducees? Surely the religious members of these sects of Judaism would gladly receive the news of a Messiah and Savior. The Pharisees above all should accept one who came not to destroy the Law but to fulfill it. (Matthew 5:17) But God did not choose the religious people. Sadly, they were more concerned about performing outward practices of piety and preserving their religion than they were about truly worshipping God. In the end, they were more interested in their political and financial agendas. To many of the Pharisees, fulfilling their view of the Law and controlling the practice of Judaism was their way to gain power and wealth. They were using religion, not seeking a relationship with God. And the Sadducees did not believe in miracles or the resurrection from the dead. Since everything about that first Christmas was a miracle of the impossible, the Sadducees disqualified themselves.

So God chose the lowly shepherds who were willing to hear the glorious gospel news. These were ordinary men leading ordinary lives, doing ordinary things on an ordinary night. I like the way Luke tells the story. First, an angel appears and announces a Savior has come into all of their <u>ordinary;</u> then came God's <u>suddenly</u>.

Suddenly, an entire army of angels from base camp Glory show up behind the lead angel and just start singing, praising, and glorifying God! All of sudden, God's glorious orchestra blasts through the heavens and his angelic choir bathes that hillside with wondrous music and light. It was a divine concert the likes of which the world had never heard.

Suddenly, the shepherd's ordinary lives are forever changed. An angel of the Lord appears. The glory of the Lord shines round about them. Literally, the entire hillside is engulfed in the glorious halo of God's light. A heavenly glory of exceeding great holiness shatters the darkness. The bright light of truth shines into the night and into their hearts. God's *"suddenly"* transforms their ordinary lives into ones of unique purpose and meaning.

And suddenly, God sets loose the angelic host–an innumerable army of angels. Their purpose is simply to praise God. "Glory to God in the highest and on earth peace, good will toward men." (Luke 2:14 KJV) It is into our ordinary that God sends the suddenly of his glorious light. When you abide in Christ, you enable God to send the suddenly of his glory, glad tidings, and good news into your life. Receive the glad tidings this Christmas and suddenly your life will be changed. Your Christmas season will be changed.

But the shepherds were more than just abiding that night in a field. They were also "keeping watch," literally on guard. They were aware of what was going on in the field. They were not asleep; what they saw was not a dream or vision. They were alert and on the job. The shepherds were not hallucinating; they all saw the same angels and were all afraid. They all heard the same angel and angelic host, for they all knew what to do. And they did it all together. Those who desire the suddenly from God to change their ordinary must also be watching and waiting for it.

The message to the shepherds was special, specific, and personal. God has a special and specific message for you this Christmas as well. It is still one of "good tidings of great joy." God has a personal Savior for you. He is Jesus.

The message to the shepherds was special because God gave them a sign by which they could find Jesus. What was the sign? Simply this: you shall find the babe wrapped in swaddling clothes, lying in a manger. The Hebrew word for manger is translated as stall, crib, or manger. Literally, it is a place where animals are kept and fed. For these shepherds, Jesus would be found lying in a place very familiar to them. They knew where to look in Bethlehem. They need not waste time checking houses or inns. Jesus would not be there. He would be found in their world—in a manger, a stall, lying in the feeding trough. It makes perfect sense to a Bethlehem shepherd: the Bread of Life came to Bethlehem, the House of Bread and was placed in a feeding crib.

The sign to the shepherds was also specific. Swaddling clothes were simple strips of cloth wrapped around a newborn to provide security, safety, and warmth. We still do it today with baby blankets for newborns—but this sign had a very specific meaning to these shepherds. It reveals who these shepherds were, why they were in the fields with sheep at night. It showed the shepherds why the angel said: a Savior Christ the Lord was born unto them!

According to Luke, the shepherds were in the fields just outside of Bethlehem: "And there were in the same country shepherds abiding in the field, keeping watch over their flock by night." (Luke 2:8 KJV) You may have read right over this verse lots of times, without giving it much thought.

But have you ever considered why the shepherds were in a field at night watching sheep? This was not a common practice for shepherds. It is not a common practice today, either. The common practice for shepherds was to bring the sheep into the "sheepfold" at night–a corral of sorts that is protected and provides safety for the sheep through the night. It has a very narrow entrance; an opening that would only allow one sheep to pass through at a time. Not very efficient for getting a herd of sheep quickly into the sheepfold, but very effective in permitting the shepherd to count the sheep as they go in one by one. Shepherds don't have a lot of responsibilities, but the number one duty of a shepherd is to not lose sheep. Shepherds keep an accurate count of the number of sheep that go into the field in the morning and how many come back to the sheepfold at night.

It is how Jesus describes the story of the lost lamb; it is at night when the shepherd is counting the sheep as they are returning to the sheepfold that he discovers one is missing. He leaves the ninety and nine, to go out at night to search for the one lost lamb. (Luke 15:1-7)

So why are the Christmas shepherds in the field and not in the sheepfold at night? There must be a specific reason. Or these must be special sheep.

The 4th-century church historian Eusebius linked the fields surrounding Bethlehem to a unique biblical location called Migdal Edar, which translated means the tower of the flock. This structure may have been constructed as a silo-type building, possibly two stories high with two floors. The top floor was open to the sky, and standing on the top floor you could see over the entire field. Clearly, this was a place to keep watch over the entire flock by night.

But the ground floor was filled with hay or straw and was the place where the birthing of lambs occurred. It would be a place of shelter from the wind and cold of the night. It was a safe place for lambs to be born. It provided protection from any wild animals that would seek to attack the baby lambs.

The first time Migdal Edar is mentioned in the Bible is in the account of Rachel, who died after giving birth to Benjamin, the youngest son of Jacob (Jacob was renamed Israel by God). "Then Israel journeyed and pitched his tent beyond the tower of Edar". (Genesis 35:21 KJV) The Jewish prophet Micah also refers to Migdal Edar. "And thou, O tower of the flock, the stronghold of the daughter of Zion, unto thee shall it come, even the first dominion; the kingdom shall come to the daughter of Jerusalem." (Micah 4:8 AKJV)

This area on the outskirts of Bethlehem is also mentioned in the Talmudic writings. According to the Talmud, all cattle found in the area surrounding Jerusalem as far as Migdal Edar were deemed to be holy and consecrated and could only be used for sacrifices in the Temple, and in particular for the peace and Passover sacrifices. There was thus a special, consecrated circle around the city of Jerusalem that reached all the way to Bethlehem.

This means the shepherds in the fields of Bethlehem that first Christmas night were not ordinary shepherds watching ordinary sheep, but these particular shepherds served the sacrificial system of the Temple. The shepherds were watching Temple sheep. These shepherds would have been specifically trained in protecting the lambs from any spot or blemish that could disqualify the lambs from use in the Temple at Passover.

These men served the Mosaic covenant, a foreshadowing of the new covenant that Jesus brings. And the flocks that they watched in the fields thirty days before Passover would have been sheep that were destined for sacrifice. But to qualify for Passover sacrifice, the little lambs born in the flock must be without spot or blemish and watched constantly for fourteen days.

When the ewe was ready to give birth, she would be brought into the ground floor of the Tower of the Flock. There, in the protection of the tower, sheltered from the wind and dangers of the open field, the ewe could give birth. Since these were Temple Sheep and their offspring were destined to be sacrificial lambs for the Passover, every precaution was taken to ensure they were without spot or blemish. The lambs born in this tower of the flock and under the watchful eye of the shepherds were then inspected and either certified by them for use as sacrifices in the temple or designated to be released for common use.

And because lambs have no wool to keep them warm when they are born, they would be wrapped in special strips of cloth–swaddling clothes. It would also protect them from getting any spot or blemish that would prevent them from serving as Passover lambs. All of this means that the "sign" given to the shepherds by the angel that night outside Bethlehem, was not just a declaration of the good news to simple shepherds; it was a powerful prophetic sign to all of Israel and to all of us. The Christ, the Savior that they are looking for, is the Lamb of God who takes away the sins of the World. He is the forever Passover Lamb.

The shepherds were not just a few guys closest to Bethlehem that the angels happen to find that first Christmas night. These Temple shepherds were charged with keeping watch over Temple sheep; for the sheep and lambs in these fields were destined for sacrifice during Passover in the Temple. These men were specially chosen by the Temple Priests to perform a very significant job: to birth and certify Passover lambs. And they were personally chosen by God to be the first to hear the revelation and to certify–to give witness–that God's permanent, sacrificial lamb had come to man in the form Christ Jesus. So it is very appropriate that the announcement of the permanent Passover lamb should be made to those who were keeping watch over the Passover lambs that provided a temporary covering. It was God's way of saying to these shepherds that salvation has come permanently and forever. Jesus is the true Passover Lamb that takes away the sins of the world.

The shepherds went to Bethlehem to certify the facts that the angel had declared: a King and Savior has been born. They went to find the one who is the Lamb of God. The one who will die on a cross to forever eradicate the penalty of death that Passover represents–the permanent payment for sin that Passover lambs could never pay.

Now we understand better what Luke records: "When they had seen him, they spread the word concerning what had been told them about this child, and all who heard it were amazed at what the shepherds said to them." (Luke 2:17–18 NIV)

These Temple shepherds–who understood their special role in assisting in the birth and certification of Passover lambs for the temple sacrifice, who understood the necessary sacrifice to cover the sins of the people–they were the ones called upon to first see the baby, first see the Christ, the Savior, and then certify to all that He is the forever Passover Lamb. They were the ones who then first proclaimed to everyone that the Christ, the Messiah, the Lamb of God had come into the world. God with us.

The angel gave them a sign because God intended them to personally act upon what they heard. They were not just looking for a baby in Bethlehem, but a baby wrapped in swaddling clothes lying in a manger. They alone understood the significance of the sign; finding this special baby lying in a manger would be unique. A baby wrapped in swaddling clothes would be what they would expect. But a baby wrapped in swaddling clothes in a manger? They knew just where to look. They did not bother to search for the King of Kings at the temple or palace or inn–all places where the world would expect him to be. They went to the stable because that is the only place in Bethlehem where you will find a baby wrapped in swaddling clothes lying in a manger.

The angel's message called the shepherds to act. God's call to service is not a time to fear. It is not a reason to fear. It will bring great joy to your life. The shepherds recognized three words in the message that had great meaning to their religious life. The angel told them of a "Savior who is Christ the Lord".

Savior meant the permanent deliverer from sin had come. No longer would the temporary sacrifices of the temple be necessary. *Christ* as translated from the Greek means "the anointed one." In Hebrew, it is the title of the Messiah. This is the one long promised and prophesied in scripture. The Lord is Adonai. It is Lord, Master, Owner. It means God himself has come.

Here is the urgency of the proclamation: Jesus is born today. Salvation is come today. The solution to your sin problem is here today. The result of this proclamation causes rejoicing. Even the angels understand what this means to a lost and dying mankind. They break forth into song: giving praise to God whose loving kindness has delivered to man the perfect, permanent salvation from sin.

And the shepherd's reaction: "Let us now go even unto Bethlehem and see this thing which is come to pass which the Lord hath made known unto us. And they came with haste...." (Luke 2:15–16 KJV). Here is why God chose the shepherds: they were willing to see and believe and go!

Notice, there was no doubt in their voice. They didn't question *if* this thing has come to pass. The shepherds believed what the angel had said. There was no doubt in their heart. There was no hesitation in their decision. With confidence, they were willing to go and see the birth of their Savior. They were willing to interrupt their lives in the middle of the night to obey God. And as we will see, joy (and Christmas spirit) come when you obey God.

But more than see and go, the shepherds became the first evangelists of the gospel message. They were willing to share the good news with others. They made known abroad what the angel told them. Note they didn't merely relate what they saw, they repeated the Word of God that had been imparted to them by the angelic messenger. The shepherds were transformed from fearful to faithful. The compelling consequence of accepting the divine message of God is that we, too, become witnesses.

It was and is the message of goodwill toward men. Literally, it is the message given to men of good will; men who are willing to cease doing evil and do good. It is a message to men who are willing to shun the wrong to do what is right. This is not some universalism that applies to all regardless of whether they know it or not, or whether they accept it or not. Although God gave the gift of salvation freely and makes it available to all, salvation is only received by those who, like the shepherds, act to receive it. We must acknowledge that Jesus is the Christ, the Son of God, and that we need God's forgiveness from our sin. We must believe in who Jesus is and confess our sin. We must personally reach out and individually receive this free gift of forgiveness from sin.

And the actions of the shepherds in sharing the good news not only passed on peace and goodwill to men, it had a dramatic effect on them as well. Consider that only the shepherds saw and heard the Heavenly host proclaim glory to God over the birth of the Savior of mankind. Only the shepherds had the opportunity to praise God with the angels. Only the shepherds could sing along with the Heavenly choir. The shepherds understood that peace on earth and goodwill to men comes only after you give glory to God in the highest. But they did not keep such a glorious event to themselves.

They "made known abroad" what they saw, heard, and experienced. Shepherds, who had no cause to share their lives with anyone, now became the first evangelists of the Gospel. What is really interesting is that the angel did not ask them to tell anyone. The instructions were simply to go and see for yourselves. But when you personally meet the Christ of Christmas, the joy of Christmas will explode in your heart. You cannot keep the spirit of Christmas to yourself. You just can't keep that kind of news to yourself. You have to go and tell someone! So on their way back to the fields and their flocks, the shepherds told everyone who would listen what they had seen and heard. They returned to their flocks rejoicing, praising, and glorifying God.

It is proof that another key to unlock the spirit of Christmas can be found in sharing the good news of Jesus birth. Share the same message the angel spoke that night so many years ago. A Savior is born! Hope has come to man. Eternal life can be received by anyone who is willing to accept and believe. God only asks that we share what we have heard and seen in our own lives. Like the blind man healed by Jesus explained: I do not know very much, but this one thing I do know. Once I was blind, then I met Jesus. Now I see! (John 9:25)

The message of Christmas has not changed from that first angelic song. This key to Christmas spirit is obtaining the everlasting joy that comes when we find the Savior and share that news with others. Inviting the Christ, the Anointed One into your heart is the first step. He is the Prince of Peace. And accepting him will bring his peace and his joy into your heart.

CHAPTER 7

NEVER LOSE THE WONDER

Luke records the reaction of the people who encountered the evangelistic message of the shepherds. "And all they that heard it wondered at those things which were told them by the shepherds." (Luke 2:18 KJV) To "wonder" means to be filled with awe at an event inexplicable by human nature; to so experience the impossible that it creates within your heart astonishment, surprise, and admiration. We marvel at the existence of such an awe-inspired occurrence and stand in wonder at the meaning.

In response to the testimony of the shepherds, "All they that heard it, wondered...." After 400 years of silence from the Old Testament to the New Testament, the first words God instructs the angel to proclaim to shepherds are "Fear not." The message of good news to all men is that no longer do you need to live in fear. I suspect those were also the first words out of the mouths of the shepherds to all who would hear. Imagine a bunch of shepherds running through your town in the middle of the night, shouting and rejoicing, and praising God! Some who heard all this commotion certainly would wonder what was happening outside their doors, and some might even be afraid. But the message of the Gospel seems to always begin with the words "Fear not."

The message the angel shared with the shepherds was to replace man's fear with great joy! No longer do we have to live in fear of death. Death no longer needs to be a fear of eternity or a fear of eternal punishment. There is permanent forgiveness. For unto you is born a Savior, Christ the Lord. Jesus was anointed by the Holy Spirit to bring deliverance to the captive, to heal the sick, and deliver the oppressed. This is the description of their Messiah: the one they were looking for to bring redemption. It is why Joseph was instructed by the angel to name him Jesus...for he shall save his people from their sin.

These people who heard the first gospel message shared by these shepherds needed a Savior. They were enslaved by the power of sin, subject to the ultimate penalty for sin, death and separation from God. But the angel delivers the good tidings, the good news. You are no longer hopelessly enslaved to sin. God has provided a Savior, which is Christ the Lord. And to that news, they were filled with wonder that first Christmas.

I can just imagine the response of Mary and Joseph as these shepherds burst into the staple. "See," they would have said one to another. "It's true! A Savior is born. There he is lying in a manger just as the angel said." I wonder if Joseph thought: *"Another angel? There's another angel delivering the news tonight? Wait a minute, who else knows what's going on here? Who else is coming over tonight?"* Go ahead, smile. You wondered about that too.

But Mary didn't wonder…she pondered. Mary kept all these things and pondered them in her heart. (Luke 2:19) To "ponder" means to bring together in one's mind; to consider. Mary was not surprised or astonished. She was not awestruck at the occurrence of the birth of Jesus. She already had been told she was to bring forth the Savior of the World. She knew the significance of Jesus' birth and her role. Her song in Luke 1:42–55 tells us of her understanding and joy at being the vessel through whom God chose to save the world.

To Mary, the arrival of the shepherds at the manger was God's confirmation that the Son of God was in her arms. Up to that moment, she and Joseph had held the knowledge of Jesus' birth in private. But now, shepherds knew! And soon the world would know.

And this is another key to unlock the spirit of Christmas in your heart: never lose the wonder! It is all too easy to treat this Christmas like the last. But take the time to wonder. Take time to ponder that once again we are celebrating the greatest gift ever given to mankind. Find a quiet moment during the season to stop, sit down, and be filled with awe at an event so inexplicable by human nature that you can only experience the impossibility it creates within your mind with astonishment, surprise, and admiration. Wonder. By all means: wonder! This gift was given by God to us, personally, permanently, and powerfully. This gift has the power to change your life forever–and personally accepting that wondrous gift with all of its wonder and awe is yet another key to unlock and rekindle the spirit of Christmas in our hearts.

CHAPTER 8

WILLING TO WORSHIP

The shepherds witnessed. The people wondered. But the wise men worshiped. The story of Christmas has different effects on different people. Some, like the shepherds, receive the good news message in faith believing and become a witness to others of what they have seen and heard. The spirit of Christmas is unlocked in their heart by seeing and sharing the good news of a Savior with others. It seems the more they witness to others about what they have seen, the more joyous their Christmas becomes.

Some people wonder in awe if such a thing could be true. Could the birth of the Messiah really have come to pass? Could the Savior really be here? Can he save even me? And if they allow themselves to be filled with the awe of such an inexplicable, inspiring, and seemingly impossible event, it can unlock joy in their heart as well.

But for some–the select few who see more than the miracle, who hear more than the message–they are the ones who give voice to the meaning. That is the story of the wise men. They come to acknowledge to the world that Jesus is not only its Savior but the King of Kings.

Matthew records the story of the wise men. Here is what he writes.

"Now when Jesus was born in Bethlehem of Judaea in the days of Herod the king, behold, there came wise men from the east to Jerusalem, Saying, Where is he that is born King of the Jews? For we have seen his star in the east, and are come to worship him. When Herod, the king, had heard these things, he was troubled, and all Jerusalem with him. And when he had gathered all the chief priests and scribes of the people together, he demanded of them where the Christ should be born. And they said unto him, In Bethlehem of Judaea; for thus it is written by the prophet, And thou Bethlehem, in the land of Judah, art not the least among the princes of Judah; for out of thee shall come a Governor that shall rule my people Israel. Then Herod, when he had privately called the wise men, inquired of them diligently what time the star appeared. And he sent them to Bethlehem and said, Go and search diligently for the young child; and when ye have found him, bring me word again, that I may come and worship

*him also. When they had heard the king, they departed;
and lo, the star, which they saw in the east, went before
them, till it came and stood over where the young child
was. When they saw the star, they rejoiced with exceeding great joy. And when they were come into the house,
they saw the young child with Mary his mother, and fell
down, and worshiped him: and when they had opened
their treasures, they presented unto him gifts: gold, and
frankincense, and myrrh. And being warned of God in a
dream that they should not return to Herod, they departed
into their own country another way."*

(MATTHEW 2:1–12 AKJV)

The story of wise men has been somewhat enhanced to present day tradition. For example, in our version of the Christmas
pageantry, we always picture the wise men coming to the manger to present their gifts. Scripturally, however, the wise men
arrived sometime after Jesus was born, since they visited him in
a house and not the manger. Also, the scripture passage doesn't
say there were just three kings, or even that they were from the
Orient, although that is the name of the Christmas carol. And
even though every Nativity set sold likely contains three wise
men and a stable, these traditions should not distract us from the
real meaning that the wise men bring to the message. These were
star-gazers, gift-givers and king worshippers.

The wise men followed a star to find Jesus, but not just any star. It was a marvelous light that God uniquely created and placed in the heavens for the wise men to see and follow. This was not just an ordinary star like the billions of others that moved in a predictable celestial orbit, but it was one that moved or stood still as God commanded! In truth, it was the unpredictable movement of this suddenly appearing star that must have captivated the attention of these wise men on the night of Jesus' birth. As we have already seen, God often brings "suddenly" into our "ordinary" to cause us to focus on what he is doing in our lives.

Who were these wise men? The term "wise men" comes from a Persian word which we would recognize as "magi." It means one who is trained or an expert in the study of the stars. We call them astronomers today. They were not astrologers as some have imagined. There is a vast difference. Astronomers are scientists who use data and observation to chart the stars of the universe in their courses. They observe and then report on and explain to us what they see. Astrologers, like palm readers and soothsayers, attempt to predict the future by using the movements of stars or their presupposed patterns. Daniel shows us these were two separate groups because when King Nebuchadnezzar of Babylon had the dream of the great image, he called for all his advisors "the magicians, and the astrologers, and the sorcerers and the Chaldeans for to show the king his dreams. So they came and stood before the king." (Daniel 2:2 KJV) Notice that the magicians (the magi) are a distinct group from the astrologers and the sorcerers.

Matthew's magi were respected advisors to a king because of their intellect and wisdom. They were considered magicians because they could read, draw what they observed, and write down their conclusions. Their abilities and reasoning were considered to be like magic compared to ordinary men. But these men were more than mere stargazers. They were likely members of a religious sect that would have advised royalty on matters of astronomy, medicine, and natural science. They believed that the appearance or disappearance of celestial objects had a corresponding relevance to the establishment or dismantling of kings and kingdoms. In other words, the appearance of a star–like the one they saw from the east–meant a new king was born.

The star that suddenly appeared in their night sky was unlike any other star they had ever observed. God commanded the star to move and stand wherever Jesus was. Before he was born, that meant wherever Mary went, the star went too. So when Mary went to visit her cousin Elizabeth in the hill country of Judea, the star would have moved to where Mary was because she was carrying Jesus inside of her. Then after months staying with Elizabeth, Mary returned to Nazareth, and the star would have moved back to stand over her. And when Mary and Joseph travel to Bethlehem, the star traveled with them until it stood over where Jesus lay in the manger.

To the magi, this star seemed to move forward and backward

in the night sky at its own will. But since these experts knew such a thing was impossible, the only other plausible explanation was that God was commanding this star to move.

They would have heard how God directed the movements of the Israelites in the wilderness: a cloud by day and a pillar of fire by night. It was common knowledge that the God of Israel opened the Red Sea and the Jordan River and allowed his people to cross over on dry ground (just ask Rahab of Jericho).

And if God directed his people with a cloud and fire, and could move the waters of rivers and seas just so his people could pass through on dry ground, it would be no great leap to believe that this same God was involved in moving a star. And if God is moving a star, that star must be worth following. Such a conclusion caused these men to interrupt their lives, leave their homes, cross a desert, and diligently follow the movement of the star for a thousand miles.

But which way do you go? You could see the star and start off in that direction, but I wonder if the magi knew more. The Old Testament prophecy of Balaam in Numbers tells of a Star that shall come out of Jacob and a scepter that shall rise out of Israel. (Numbers 24:17) You will recall that Balaam was an unscrupulous soothsayer who was hired by the King of Moab to pronounce a curse upon Israel, but in the end could only bless Israel and did so seven times. And the curse God did give him to pronounce, prophesied the downfall of Moab! It was physically fulfilled by King David (2 Samuel 8:2), but at the same time God intended it as a sign for the magi of the coming Messiah. Since Balaam lived in Mesopotamia, near the Euphrates River, I wonder if the magi may have heard of Balaam's story–it is hard to forget a talking donkey–and remembered that the star represented the rising of a King of Israel. Certainly, that would have put them on the path to Judea.

While the scriptures tell us only of the wise men and the star, anyone who looked into the heavens during that first Christmas could have seen that star, too. They would have seen the star move, stop, and back-up, yet only the wise men left what they were doing to follow the star to Jesus. Perhaps the other people who saw the star lacked the training to understand its significance.

But perhaps, they were simply too busy with their own lives to stop and take more than casual notice. It can happen to us, though. At best we may only be giving God casual notice in our lives. We can get so busy with the doing of Christmas that we fail to take the time to simply look up to Heaven and rejoice at this great thing that has come to pass in our life. But as God created a unique star and placed it in the heavens for the wise men, he is still desiring to guide us in the pathways he has planned for our everyday walk. If we will look to him in faith, he will guide us and we will hear him say: *This is the way, walk ye in it.* (Isaiah 30:21)

It was the presence of that star–it's appearing and re-appearing–that caused the wise men to rejoice with exceeding great joy! Just seeing the star and knowing God's hand was moving it gave them great joy. The trip must have been one of pronounced excitement each day. The star's appearance each night had to encourage their hearts to know they were walking in the right direction.

Notice that the wise men had to walk by faith during the day; only at night could they see the star and have their faith reassured that their steps were walking in the right direction. To them the star became a symbol of God's presence in their life, and God's confirmation that they were walking according to his purpose for them. They had already determined when they left home their one purpose was to find the newborn king and worship him. They sought not just the Savior but the King. It was the joy in seeing the star that kept the wise men going to find the newborn king.

However, the wise men's journey was not without danger and dead-ends. As they traveled to the west and neared Jerusalem, it must have occurred to them that the newborn king was King of the Jews. The appropriate course for these royal advisors then would be to present themselves to the King in Jerusalem. Perhaps this was his son who was born, but if not, certainly the ruler would know all of the goings on of his kingdom–or he should know.

What the wise men did not know was who they were addressing. Herod the Great was third generation ruler of that land. His grandfather had been made governor by the Romans; his father had been appointed procurator of Judea by the Romans. And Herod the Great had been appointed by none other than Mark Anthony to be tetrarch of all Galilee. The Roman Senate had approved his kingship in 40 BC, provided Herod could gain control of Palestine by force. He did. Ruthlessly.

He besieged Jerusalem and conquered it in 37 BC. He used the force of the Roman Army to establish and enforce his tyrannical rule, killing, murdering, or massacring all those who stood in his way. He killed one of his wives, three of his sons, and anyone else who threatened his being king.

While Herod's family was actually from Edom (south of Israel), he considered himself a Jew–or at least Jewish enough to convince Rome he was the right man for the job. Herod was a descendant of Esau, the older brother of Jacob. Jacob was the father of twelve sons, the tribes of Israel. Jacob's descendants, not Esau's, were the ones whom God chose to receive fulfilment of God's covenant with Abraham, Isaac, and Jacob.

By increasing the splendor of Jerusalem and the Temple (at an incalculable cost, Herod beautified the Temple with white marble, gold, and jewels), he paid enough lip service to convince the real Jews he was worth keeping. Yet it was his conniving and cruelty that troubled Jerusalem; for when Herod found out the wise men believed there was another king of the Jews, his murderous temper troubled everyone. Herod saw Jesus as a threat. Jerusalem saw Jesus as trouble. Only the wise men saw Jesus as a King worthy of worship.

Although before the arrival of the wise men to Jerusalem, Herod could have looked out his window and seen the star, once the wise men reached Jerusalem, I think God hid the star from view. Herod had no clue where this rival king would be born. Ironically, everyone but Herod knew the answer. Once Herod was informed of the place by the chief priests and scribes, he only needed to know the time of the star's appearing in order to determine how old the child was and how imminent the threat to his kingdom.

Herod called the wise men back, privately, because he did not want Jerusalem to know his evil plan. He pressed them for answers to his questions so he could determine how old this threat to his kingdom was. Then he veiled his plan in religion, promising the wise men that he too wanted to worship this new king.

But it was all his evil plot. The slaughter of all the children of Bethlehem under the age of two shows the depths of the depravity this servant of Satan had reached. Of course God knew what Herod was planning. He sent an angel to safely usher Joseph, Mary, and Jesus out of Bethlehem to Egypt, after the wise men had visited and returned to their homeland without informing Herod. Make no mistake, this was not some coincidental murderous act by an insane and jealous king. It was a direct attempt by the devil to thwart the redemptive plan of God by killing Jesus as a baby. But he isn't that powerful, and God's plans are never thwarted. God always wins.

As royal advisors, the wise men knew the proper protocols to follow when entering another king's domain. The visitation with Herod may have been politically correct, but in the end it was an unending nightmare for hundreds of people in Bethlehem. Even still, the knowledge gained by Herod to estimate the age of the new king and his despicable act of murder fulfilled what was prophesied by Jeremiah hundreds of years before. (Jeremiah 31:15) And though they had detoured into a dead end with Herod, as soon as they left Jerusalem, they rejoiced with exceeding great joy when God caused the star to reappear and again direct their path.

The wise men followed the star with one purpose in their hearts: worship! But notice how they approached the King of Kings. The order of their approach is important to understanding the proper worship of the king. First, they presented themselves. Then they personally worshiped. Then they presented their gifts.

In presenting themselves, Matthew records they 'fell down" or more accurately, they bowed down. This is the only way to begin worship of the King of Kings. We must change our position, humble ourselves, and recognize he is great in our life. From this prostrated position of humility, these wise men, who have allowed the very presence of God direct their path, who have found great joy and rejoicing in the presence of God's star, are ready to worship.

And it is only after they have humbled themselves and

worshiped that they presented their gifts of gold, frankincense, and myrrh. Each gift acknowledged who Jesus was and what he came to do. Each gift tells us of the purpose of Christmas. Each gift also symbolizes an important part of how God wants us to live our lives before him. Therefore, we need to look carefully at each gift and apply their lessons to our hearts this Christmas season.

Gold is a precious metal–so highly valued that it has formed the foundation of the world's economic system. It is a measure of success, power, and royalty. Pure gold is not an alloy–that is, a substance resulting from the combination of metals. It is an element in itself. It is a base element on the Periodic Table of Elements. Nothing is added to it to make it gold. It does not need to be embellished to give it value. It has intrinsic value. It represents purity and royalty. It was given to Jesus to acknowledge his royal ancestry and his prophesied purpose in coming–he will rule the world from King David's throne forever. He is the King of all Kings.

The gift of gold is also a lesson to us that our lives should be pure before God. We should let God have first place in our hearts and lives. God should be the foundation upon which our world is built. The measure of our success should be God's purest standard, Jesus. And he should be in the center of our lives. By living our lives in purity before him, we enable the true spirit of Christmas to be produced in our hearts.

Frankincense is a sweet smelling perfume, but its aroma

is only smelled when it is burned with fire. It was given by the wise men as a worship offering. The aroma is so pungent that it permeates the atmosphere of the room into which it is released. Its fragrance can change the atmosphere in a room. Thus we should offer our worship to God in a pure offering. We should allow the Holy Spirit to burn within us so that the sweet perfume of worship can rise upward unto God. And as we worship, we will see the spirit of Christmas fill our hearts and then fill the atmosphere around us. The sweetness seen in our lives becomes the aroma of Christmas smelled by those who we encounter. Worship will release the spirit of Christmas in our lives and the spirit of Christmas will change the atmosphere in our home.

Myrrh is an antiseptic used in New Testament times in preparation for burial. The gift foretold of Jesus' purpose in coming–to die for our sins and thereby offer us eternal life. He came to be our Savior. But the lesson applies even deeper than acknowledging the saving grace of Jesus. As antiseptic works to kill the germs which bring infection, disease, and death, so too must we allow God to cleanse our lives of the disease of sin and the sinful germs that have infected our lives. For those who believe, the Bible affords cleansing just by reading it. It can wash away the sinful dust we collect in our lives by walking through the world. But dusty germs that we allow to stay on our lives produce sinful infection in our lives. That sin needs the antiseptic of God's gift of salvation. Accepting his gift of Jesus will eradicate all of the sinful infection and disease. It is the only way. There is no other cure for sin.

Because the wise men gave gifts to the Christ child, we too give gifts to each other at Christmas. And this tradition typically generates the question: "*What do you want for Christmas?* Rarely do they ask: "*What do you need for Christmas?*"

There is a big difference between what we truly need and what we want. Often, we get into trouble because we chase after our wants, rather than focusing first on what we need. And we can easily fall into the trap and miss seeing Christmas because we are focused only on what we want (and didn't get), rather than what we truly need. What the wise men presented were gifts God determined were the ones we needed to see and what God knew needed to be given.

After the wise men presented themselves, their worship, and their gifts, they departed back to their own country (without telling Herod, just as they were instructed by God to do). While the story of the wise men is full of miraculous events, what is truly intriguing is that they are the only gentiles invited to the Christmas story! It means that all are welcome to come to the Christmas story. Christmas is not just a special time for Christians. God intends it to be a celebration for all mankind.

What the wise men were focused on that first Christmas is what God wants us to focus on every day. It is what produces the true spirit of Christmas in our hearts: worship. We should worship at the thought that our Savior has come. We should worship because our sins have been forgiven. We should worship because by accepting Jesus we have eternal life! It was his coming, his living, his dying for our sins, and his resurrection to life that gives all of the real meaning to Christmas. We should worship because our King of Kings is in heaven and is soon to return. The wise men came and found the young child, but saw the King of Kings and Lord of Lords! And that is what wise men focus on at Christmas.

CHAPTER 9

THAT NEEDFUL THING

Christmas dinner. If two words in the English language ever had the power to simultaneously produce delight and depression in the hearts of those who hear the words, these two words possess the power. To the partaker, the words *Christmas dinner* evoke pleasant thoughts of turkey or glazed ham, twice-baked potatoes, green bean casseroles and delectable desserts (or whatever your favorite Christmas dinner foods are). It's Thanksgiving dinner all over again.

But to the person tasked with preparing the Christmas feast, the words *Christmas dinner* provoke memories of numerous hours spent in the kitchen baking that ham, twice baking those potatoes, and rolling out the pastry for those desserts. Casseroles just don't make themselves. It's Thanksgiving dinner all over again!

Depending on which side of the table you start from, Christmas dinner can cause you to lose whatever Christmas spirit you've been keeping. There must be a key to unlock the keeping of Christmas joy through Christmas dinner.

I found a Christmas dinner story in the Bible that will help us unlock Christmas spirit through Christmas dinner. Okay, it's not exactly a Christmas dinner bible story, since Christmas as a holiday had not yet been invented during Jesus' life on earth. But if we can take a little liberty to draw a parallel between Jesus' coming as a baby in a manger, and his coming to dinner with his disciples during his ministry, I believe we will see all of the elements of preparing a Christmas dinner. And in seeing those elements and how Jesus dealt with them, we will discover another key to unlocking the Christmas spirit in our homes at Christmas dinner.

We have to visit the house of Martha in the village of Bethany, just outside of Jerusalem on this one particular evening. Although this dinner occurred thousands of years ago, and well before Christmas dinners existed, if this story was placed in any home in December, it would aptly describe any Christmas dinner scene today. This Christmas dinner story is in Luke 10: 38–42.

This is still a story about preparing for the arrival of Jesus, just like Mary and Joseph had to do. But this story is about Mary and Martha (the ones who had a brother named Lazarus). And if you've ever been in a kitchen where a Christmas dinner is being prepared, you can easily envision the goings on between Mary and Martha. Here is the story:

"Now it came to pass, as they went, that he entered into a certain village: and a certain woman named Martha received him into her house. And she had a sister called Mary, which also sat at Jesus' feet, and heard his word. But Martha was cumbered about much serving, and came to him, and said, Lord, dost thou not care that my sister hath left me to serve alone? Bid her therefore that she help me.

And Jesus answered and said unto her, Martha, Martha, thou art careful and troubled about many things. But one thing is needful, and Mary hath chosen that good part, which shall not be taken away from her."

(LUKE 10:38–42 KJV)

For those not readily familiar with this Christmas story, here is a little background. From John's gospel we learn the "certain village" is Bethany, a small town on the eastern slope of the Mount of Olives, about 2 miles from Jerusalem, and on the road to Jericho. Martha has a house here. Her name means "lady of the house" or "mistress". Her gifting is hospitality. She was the one who would meet, welcome, and serve the guests invited into her home. Martha loved to entertain.

Martha's sister was Mary. Her brother was named Lazarus (the one whom Jesus raised from the dead.) Mary and Lazarus apparently lived with Martha. All three were close friends of Jesus. They were also disciples and followers of Jesus. And when Jesus and his twelve disciples were nearby, they occasionally came to stay with Martha. Mary seemed to have a contemplative spirit; her love for Jesus motivated her to sit at his feet and listen to his every word. Now, I don't want you to get the wrong impression about Martha; she loved Jesus too. It's just that her way of worshiping Jesus was to do what she did best–hospitality and service.

And here is where we find the point of this Christmas dinner story. Martha, having invited Jesus and twelve of his closest disciples in for dinner, is now busily preparing a meal. Think of it in terms of preparing Christmas dinner for the family. She's running around the kitchen adding water to the soup, rolling out the bread. She's checking on the turkey in the oven. I can just envision her saying: "Oh, what's that pie that Jesus likes so much?" It's in her nature to please her friends and guests with the best that she can make. And it is her desire to please Jesus with her hospitality and dinner.

The King James Version of the Bible describes her activity in verse 40: "But Martha was *cumbered about* with much serving" (emphasis added). The New International Version translates this verse: "But Martha was *distracted* by all the preparations that had to be made" (emphasis added). Martha was cumbered. She was over-burdened. She was being dragged down, consumed by the enormity of the task. She was distracted in all her doing for the guests. But this is what she chose to do! This is her calling; her forte. She invited Jesus in and now was in the midst of making the meal into a Martha Stewart feast to perfection.

She had already decided what Jesus needed. She didn't ask; she just presumed what Jesus needed. And when her preparations became more than she alone could bear, she looked for some help. She looked and saw her sister, Mary, just sitting there! She was sitting at the feet of Jesus just listening. Mary was doing nothing! Martha had allowed the pressures of the preparations she had devised to poison her attitude toward Mary. Her motives were originally pure. Like Mary, she wanted to worship Jesus the best way she knew how.

But now, how could she worship! How could Mary just sit there? Martha is to the point of tears. It was all falling apart; all of Martha's plans, her preparations, her perfections were about to result in failure. So she speaks to Jesus. Surely, he can see the importance of what she is trying to do and get Mary to help!

Look how Martha phrases the question to Jesus. "Lord, don't you care that my sister has left me to do the work by myself? Tell her to help me!" (Luke 10:40 NIV) Have you ever noticed that when we get into trouble (whether by our own making or not), our first complaint to God *is don't you care, God?* It is as if we believe God's job is to make our lives perfect and trouble-free. And when difficulties and hardship come our way, we somehow conclude that God must not care for us, otherwise this trouble would not have happened. We need to remember what Jesus told his disciples: "… In the world you will have tribulation: but be of good cheer, I have overcome the world." (John 16:33 NKJV) Jesus warned us our lives would encounter the pressure, oppression, stress, anguish, adversity, affliction, and distress of tribulation. And sometimes, like Martha, we manufacture our own–even at Christmas.

Martha even took it up a notch; for she made it all about herself. It wasn't just that she was having trouble getting the meal together, it was that her sister's failure to help her was the cause of her trouble. So, in her frustration Martha rationalized: *Jesus should make her help me, because it's all about what I need, my plans, my dinner, and what I am doing!*

But seeing the heart of each woman, Jesus tenderly speaks to Martha. He recognizes Martha's work and helps her understand how it has affected her: she is distressed, distracted, and disappointed. In responding to Martha's plea, Jesus puts the two choices into proper perspective. Jesus points out that Mary's choice to listen to Jesus is the better choice. While what Martha has chosen to do is nice, it is not needful.

When Christmas comes this season, will you be so wrapped up in the preparations that you reach the point of distress? It is easy to do. With all of the pressures to make the perfect Christmas memory for the family, we can become "cumbered" like Martha. It can happen without notice.

We woke up late (because we were up late wrapping presents). Opening the presents took longer than expected (we bought too many, which is why we were up so late wrapping.) Now the guests will be here in a couple of hours, the ham needs to go in the oven, the potatoes need to be made. Who is doing the vegetables? Why won't they stop playing with those toys and help! It quickly builds up stress and we lose whatever spirit of Christmas we had.

How will you prepare for Christ's coming to your home? The secret is shared by Jesus in verse 42: Just relax. Find that one thing that is *needful...and do that thing!* You see, for all the tinsel and colored lights, the Christmas presents and bows, the Christmas dinner and family gathering, the needful thing Jesus wants is our worship. Jesus is looking for wise men and women who will come to him and worship. And he wants us to fellowship one with another in that same spirit of praise and worship for the day. It is another key to Christmas spirit: focus on just what is needful and let go of all of the rest that is nice but not needful. Find that thing (the tradition, memory, or experience) that speaks Christmas spirit to your family and do that thing to the best of your ability.

CHAPTER 10

NEVER TOO OLD FOR CHRISTMAS

Christmas is for kids, or so some contend. The faith expressed by children in the awe and wonder of Christmas decorations, in the excitement and anticipation of Christmas day certainly support the contention. Children can and often do enjoy Christmas morning more than the adults. Those who hold such belief likely base the lack of enjoyment by the adults on the reality that adults have long since given up believing in Santa Claus.

The irony, of course, is that Santa Claus is himself a storybook fiction that parents have read to their children as tradition. We parents have implanted the notion into our children of a mythical, gift-giving elf visiting houses in one night to leave gifts under the tree. Santa Claus is a figment of our imaginative creation: so when we grow up, we learn that Santa Claus isn't real. He is just for kids. And likewise, for some, Christmas isn't real. It is just for kids too.

Fortunately, God's Christmas story is not age-dependent. In fact, God purposefully planted two senior saints–Simeon and Anna–into the Christmas story so that we would know God believes you are never too old for Christmas! These two saints of God appear in Luke's gospel at the end of Chapter 2. Their stories remind us that the spirit of Christmas is for young and old alike. Here is their story, beginning at Luke 2:25.

"And, behold, there was a man in Jerusalem, whose name was Simeon; and the same man was just and devout, waiting for the consolation of Israel: and the Holy Ghost was upon him. And it was revealed unto him by the Holy Ghost, that he should not see death before he had seen the Lord's Christ. And he came by the Spirit into the temple: and when the parents brought in the child Jesus, to do for him after the custom of the law, Then took he him up in his arms, and blessed God, and said, Lord, now lettest thou thy servant depart in peace, according to thy word: For mine eyes have seen thy salvation, Which thou hast prepared before the face of all people; A light to lighten the Gentiles, and the glory of thy people Israel. And Joseph and Mary marveled at those things which were spoken of him. And Simeon blessed them, and said unto Mary his

mother, Behold, this child is set for the fall and rising again of many in Israel; and for a sign which shall be spoken against; (Yea, a sword shall pierce through thy own soul also,) that the thoughts of many hearts may be revealed."

(LUKE 2:25–35 KJV)

"And there was one Anna, a prophetess, the daughter of Phanuel, of the tribe of Aser: she was of a great age, and had lived with an husband seven years from her virginity; And she was a widow of about fourscore and four years, which departed not from the temple, but served God with fastings and prayers night and day. And she coming in that instant gave thanks likewise unto the Lord, and spake of him to all them that looked for redemption in Jerusalem."

(LUKE 2:36–38 KJV)

Simeon's story is special because it is completely Holy Spirit directed. What we know of Simeon is that he was 'just and devout'–just before men and devout before God. In other words, he was in right standing before God and in right relation with all men. In and of itself, that is a laudable commentary on anyone's life.

He believed the Messiah was coming–it is what "waiting for the consolation of Israel" means. Simeon was looking forward with great anticipation to that time when Israel would be comforted (consoled) by the coming of its Messiah–the consolation of Israel. Just like the exiled Jews of the Old Testament looked forward to the comfort they would enjoy at being restored to their land by the divine act of consolation, so Simeon eagerly looked forward to his Messiah.

But more than mere lip service, Simeon's entire life had been grounded with this belief. Simeon believed in the coming of the Messiah. And more than that, he believed the Messiah would come in his lifetime. It is one thing to hold a belief in the appearance of the divine promise, only to give up and forget it when the fulfillment is not soon forthcoming. But for Simeon, he grasped tightly to the promise of the Messiah. It captivated his thoughts. It filled his conversation. His heart was filled with the hope and expectation that the Messiah could come in his day.

Because Simeon chose to believe in the coming of the Messiah, the Holy Spirit was upon him. The Holy Spirit came not just as a spirit of holiness but also as a spirit of prophecy. This is no small thing. Before the Day of Pentecost in Acts Chapter 2, only three types of people in the Bible were normal recipients of the power of the Holy Spirit: prophets, priests, and kings. Occasionally, though, God would pour out His Holy Spirit upon those who were not in the typical class; because God had a special purpose for them to fulfill, and they needed a special power to fulfill it. Simeon was that kind of guy; he had a special God-directed purpose.

Simeon's life (like we shall see with Anna's in a moment) had been selected for one culminating purpose: to be a witness to the world that the Messiah had come in flesh. The Bible sets a standard that for a thing to be established, it must have two to three witnesses. (Deut. 19:15; Matthew 18:16). We do the same in our court system. We require the testimony of more than one witness to confirm a fact. In order to be a witness you must tell others your story. The shepherds were the first witnesses; Simeon was the second; Anna was the third. Each testified that this child was Messiah, Christ, the Savior of the world. Three independent, unrelated, and credible witnesses who saw the same child and delivered the same testimony.

Because of Simeon's devotion to God, his life was not only Spirit-filled, it was Spirit-directed. He allowed the Holy Spirit to guide his life. His steps were divinely ordered steps. He followed the leading the Holy Spirit in every aspect of his life. The characteristics that mark his life are summed up in the words *just* and *devout.*

But it was not only his steps that were directed. The presence of the Holy Spirit upon Simeon's life meant that his words were Spirit–given. As a prophet, he spoke the words God gave him to speak. He did not speak his opinion, but prophetic fact. Therefore, Simeon was given divinely–revealed knowledge.

Like the prophet Samuel, I believe God was with Simeon so that none of his words fell to the ground. (1 Samuel 3:19) I believe every word Simeon spoke under the unction of the Holy Spirit was honored and performed by God. This was essential for the purpose God had called Simeon to. For the people to believe his word on the day he saw Jesus, they had to believe the truth of his words every day.

God promised Simeon the desire of his heart–to see the Messiah. The Holy Spirit specifically told Simeon he would not die until he had seen the Messiah. According to the Word of God, Simeon waited for the revelation of the Messiah. He spent his whole life waiting for one event; one glorious, life-affirming event. And God made sure this senior saint was alive to see what his heart believed–the true spirit of Christmas.

Because Simeon's steps were spirit–directed, it is not surprising that the Holy Spirit would lead him to the Temple on the very day that Mary and Joseph present Jesus for dedication at the Temple in Jerusalem. We will always encounter God when we obediently follow the steps he has directed because they always lead us to the place where he is.

Because he was full of the Holy Spirit, Simeon's steps were ordered directly to where Mary and Joseph stood, and Simeon instantly recognized the Messiah in the arms of Mary. He had never met the couple. He did not have a sign like the shepherds. But in his heart, in his spirit, he bore witness that this child was Messiah. This is the one he had waited his whole life for. So Simeon can exclaim, *I'm ready for death for I have seen my Savior!* You are only ready to depart this world through death's door after you have met Christ and accepted his salvation.

Holding Jesus in his arms, Simeon testifies to who this child is and what he has come to do. It is an important testimony. To the common Jew of his day, the Messiah was to be the one who would conquer the Romans, overthrow their government and occupation, and set up his kingdom. Messiah was coming to Israel to establish their preeminence of power over all the Gentile nations; to rule and reign as prophesied by the Old Testament prophets.

Unfortunately, the Jews got a little ahead of themselves. Messiah will come to rule and reign, just not yet. That is for his second coming. His first coming is as a servant, submitted to the Father's work. The first coming of the Messiah is to conquer sin and death, and that requires a suffering servant, the man of sorrows as Isaiah 53 prophesies.

Simeon's purpose is to set his misguided, fellow Jews straight. He testifies that salvation has come to all people. Light has come to the gentiles and that light will bring glory to Israel. In other words, the purpose of Messiah's first coming is not to conquer Rome or reestablish Israel as a world power, but to conquer sin and death. Simeon is a witness to the Savior.

But there is one more highlight to Simeon's story. God not only fulfilled His promise by letting Simeon *see* the Messiah, but God graciously allowed Simeon to **hold** the Messiah! You see, God always delivers on his promises, and his grace abounds to give even more than we can ask or think. Simeon is so overjoyed at the graciousness and faithfulness of God that he Blesses God, for his Savior has come.

Then we have Anna, another senior saint of God. A widow

who has devoted the last eighty-four years of her life to serving God in the Temple. Anna was a prophetess so, like Simeon, the power of the Holy Spirit was upon her. She also speaks prophetic fact. Because she was continually in the temple, she was continually in the presence of God.

As a prophetess she spoke the word of God in truth, and God honored the word she spoke to make it come to pass every single time. She, too, had been specially selected by God to be a third witness to the true purpose of Jesus coming–to be the Savior of the sinner. She continually stayed in the presence of God, and I believe God was present with her. She is an example that regardless of age, we are never too old to serve God. And we are never too old to experience the presence and power of God in our life.

Her purpose was also God–directed. For in the same instant that Simeon is holding Jesus and declaring salvation to the world, Anna walks up and begins to corroborate the witness of Simeon. To all who will listen, she testifies of the redemption of Jerusalem through this baby.

Some may look at Anna's life and offer pity, seeing a life marred by the tragic death of her husband after only seven short years of marriage. They would bemoan a widowed life, destitute and resigned to servitude in the Temple. Yet if Anna were standing next to them, I believe she'd smack them upside their punk'in-shaped heads.

For what Anna knows, what Simeon knows, what all senior saints know, is that a life spent in service to others is the highest and best form of godly life to live. It is the highest purpose we can accomplish. The greatest rewards come to those who have given their lives to serve God by serving others. No one would dare criticize Mother Theresa for the life she chose in service to others. Those whom she touched and ministered to continually sing her praise.

Many do not understand a life of such devotion as we see in Simeon and Anna. But, there are things in this world that are learned not by books or conferred by degrees of higher education. These truths come only by years of experience. God preserved the lives of Simeon and Anna for one divinely appointed, God directed purpose—seeing the Messiah and proclaiming the purpose of his coming.

Senior saints know that God keeps his word. God is faithful. He will never give up on you. Senior saints know that God's blessings are always greater than we can think. They know that God is a giver because his love is so great. Senior saints know because they have lived a faith-filled life proven true by experience.

Senior saints know that death is a departure, not a dead end. Death is only to be feared by those who have not seen and accepted the Savior. But to those, like Simeon and Anna, who have seen and received Jesus as their savior, they have no fear of death. They know the words of Jesus: "I will come again and receive you unto myself; that where I am, there ye may be also." (John 14:3 KJV)

And in these two senior saints, we find another key to unlock

Christmas spirit–you are never too old to celebrate the coming of Christ at Christmas. Don't let the world convince you that your time for joy is past; that your best days are behind you. Do not be dissuaded from celebrating Christmas. You can prove them all wrong by celebrating Christmas with all the energy you can muster. In fact, let the abounding joy you feel in your heart energize you to celebrating Christmas to its fullest extent. That'll show 'em–you're never too old for Christmas!

CHAPTER 11

EXPECTING CHRISTMAS

To live your whole life righteously before God and man, yet be denied the one thing you desire most above all else–a child–is a difficult thing to bear. This is especially difficult at Christmas when the entire day seems to be about children and family. But for Zachariah and Elizabeth, their season for having children had passed. They were now very old and well past child-bearing years. Though they had prayed and prayed, no child had been born to them. Though they could not understand why God did not answer their prayers, they did not let their unanswered prayer stop them from living for God.

They walked in righteousness–in right standing–before God, and they walked blameless–without fault–before their fellow man. Zachariah and Elizabeth observed all of God's commandments and regulations to the point that no one could find fault with their relationship to God or in their relationship with others.

Here is how Luke begins their story.

> *"In the days when Herod was king of Judea there was a certain priest whose name was Zachariah, of the daily service (the division) of Abia; and his wife was also a descendant of Aaron, and her name was Elizabeth. And they both were righteous in the sight of God, walking blamelessly in all the commandments and requirements of the Lord. But they had no child, for Elizabeth was barren; and both were far advanced in years."*
>
> (LUKE 1:5-7 AMP)

Luke reports that they were–in the observance of God's laws and regulations–blameless.

In other words, not one man could find fault with the way they lived. This is not some perfection of saintly living: they were just like you and me. They were blameless in their relationship before men because they were not just observant of God's laws; they lived out God's laws in the purity of their hearts, in their conversation, and in their actions before men. They did not just believe it in their hearts or talk about it in their conversations, they lived out their faith every day before all men.

Zachariah and Elizabeth were living examples of King Solomon's admonition: "Train up a child in the way he should go: and when he is old, he will not depart from it." (Proverbs

22:6 NKJV) They walked in God's ordinances, and as it relates to worship, they let every breath praise the Lord. They were in that regard: worship-walkers. Everything they said and did demonstrated their reverence for and obedience to God. They walked blamelessly before men because they allowed their daily worship to affect their daily lives. They worshiped God not just in their word and deed, but also in their heart. How they worshipped came out in how they walked before God and men.

Both Zachariah and Elizabeth were descendants of Aaron, the first High Priest of Israel. Zachariah was a priest of the priestly division of Abijah. (King David had divided the priesthood into twenty-four divisions or courses in accordance with the descendants of Aaron. Each division had an appointed time to come to the Temple and perform their priestly duties for one course or period of time, likely a week.)

But for all their righteous and faithful devotion to God, they still did not receive the sought-after answer to their solitary prayer: to have a child. What is remarkable and instructive to us is that they did not allow this unanswered prayer to deter them from living for God.

Some may have used this as an excuse to doubt God or to stop serving God altogether. But Zachariah and Elizabeth did not blame God. They did not turn against God. They did not reject God because he didn't answer their prayers immediately when they prayed.

In fact, it was quite the opposite. Zachariah and Elizabeth lived out their devotion to God in front of everyone they met, in spite of the glaring barrenness in their lives. And because we have the blessing of knowing their whole story, as we shall see, God was not denying their prayers for a child. He was merely delaying answering their prayers for the time that best fit his plans and purposes for delivery of the greatest gift man has ever received: Jesus.

Paul told us that Jesus, God's only Son, came to this world "when the fullness of the time was come...." (Galatians 4:4 KJV) Our timing is not always God's timing. But God is always on-time, every time. What Zachariah and Elizabeth did not yet know was that God was preparing for Christmas. God specially chose Zachariah and Elizabeth, and they had an important role to play in the coming of the Savior. And that meant Zachariah and Elizabeth had to wait until God said it was time. God does not always answer prayers with a "yes" or "no." Sometimes, it is a "not yet." Sometimes it is silence.

While it may have seemed to Zachariah and Elizabeth that the answer to their prayer for a child was "no," God's answer was really "not yet." In the meantime, they had to walk by faith–just like the rest of us–believing God is still there. They had to keep believing God answered prayer, even though they saw no answer to this prayer. They had to keep believing God still loved them and he was worth serving even if he did not answer this prayer. Walking by faith and trusting God did not necessarily make their childless circumstances any easier to bear, but trusting God did give them hope and someone to hold on to.

By today's standards being childless may not be as great a burden. In fact, for a myriad of reasons many couples in our society choose not to have children. But 2,000 years ago, in the Hebrew society of Zachariah and Elizabeth, being childless was a reproach. People talked. People said you were cursed by God. The righteous living of Zachariah and Elizabeth in the face of their barrenness would appear to be hypocritical. How could they fulfill the commandments of God in Deuteronomy 6 and teach the Law to their children if they had none? Zachariah's neighbors had to question how a priest in the Temple can claim to be in right standing with God if he has not been blessed with children.

As the Psalmist said: "Lo, children are an heritage of the LORD: and the fruit of the womb is his reward. As arrows are in the hand of a mighty man; so are children of the youth. Happy is the man that hath his quiver full of them: they shall not be ashamed...." (Psalms 127:3–5 KJV) But without children, Zachariah and Elizabeth knew what that shame felt like.

When you live in a time and community where having children is not only expected but interpreted as a direct blessing of God, not being able to have children is a grievous burden to bear.

Elizabeth certainly felt the brunt of this burden: in Israel, her very identity as a godly Jewish woman was defined by her ability to have children. Every day, Elizabeth had to suffer under the weight of scornful glances and half-heard whispers. She was the one they called barren. The Hebrew word for barren is *akarah* meaning bereaved of children, deprived. It carries the agricultural connotation of being uprooted, torn away from the family stock, left to wither without progeny, and a pitiful land that bears no crop.

And it was not just the strangers. Elizabeth had to constantly deal with all of her friends and family as well. Every child born to a relative was a reminder that she was unfruitful. Yet, through the time of her natural child-bearing years, she is barren.

It was the desire of every Jewish girl to raise-up a family for God. It wasn't as if Elizabeth could be a professional woman, go to work each day, and devote herself to a career. Her society had no such jobs for women. She was the wife of a priest of the Temple. Her role was to stay at home and raise the family. Without a family to raise, she just stayed at home.

There can be no doubt that like Samuel's mother Hannah, Elizabeth prayed and wept before the Lord, begging for a child. I am sure Zachariah likewise prayed, day after day, month after month, year after year. And still, no child was born to them.

It is hard to understand why God does not immediately answer every earnest prayer we pray. This unanswered prayer is equally difficult for Elizabeth's husband Zachariah; he is a priest of God. If God should be attuned to anyone at all when it comes to answering prayer, it should be one of his priests. And through the season when Zachariah and Elizabeth should be having children, but do not, it can cause a crisis of faith.

Is God real? Does he hear my prayers? They prayed and sought the Lord for a child, and although it appeared the answer was no, Zachariah and Elizabeth did not allow that unanswered prayer to challenge their faith in God. They still believed God was real. They still chose to believe God answers prayer. They still lived righteously according to the Word of God they had received. They still lived blameless before men. They still remained steadfast in their faith, even though they may not have understood why God chose not to answer their prayer in their season.

Perhaps once the season for child-bearing had passed, they thought the answer must have been "no." It becomes understandable. We think to ourselves: *Well, I guess God did not want me to have children.* And then our prayers can turn a little bitter: *God if you had only allowed me to have children, I would have been a great parent.*

In these prayers, we forget that God has an infinite number of ways to answer our prayers. Sometimes God's answer to our prayer is: *Not yet. I'm working out my divine plan and you are a part of it. I know it hurts, but if you can just wait just a little while longer, I promise the wait will be worth it all.*

In our prayers, we often forget to account for God's perspective. He is working out his sovereign will in our lives, and in the lives of those around us. In fact, often those around us may very well be a part of that plan and essential to the answer to our prayers.

Think about it. God's plan for Zachariah and Elizabeth was to give them a son who had a special role to play in God's redemptive plan. He would be the forerunner of Christ. So to answer Zachariah's and Elizabeth's prayer, God was waiting for Mary to be born, grow up, become the beautiful woman of God, and be willing to be the one he could use to miraculously bring a Savior into the world through the virgin birth.

Then God was waiting for Joseph to notice Mary, get up enough nerve to talk to her, fall in love with her, and ask her to be his wife. God was orchestrating all of these events in Mary and Joseph's life.

And Zachariah and Elizabeth had to wait for all that to happen too. But most importantly, Elizabeth's impossible pregnancy–when she was old and past all child-bearing years–was the sign the angel Gabriel announced to Mary that the virgin birth of Christ in her was also God making the impossible become possible. It was all part of God's perfect timing.

I believe God heard Elizabeth's very first prayer for a child. And in that moment, God had to say: *Elizabeth, I love you, but you have to wait because I've chosen you for something special.* The difficulty for Elizabeth is that God didn't say that directly to her. He said it in his silence to her prayer. Why? Because God knew they would continue to serve him, even if the answer to their prayer did not come right away. Because God chose them, and God wanted to see them walk in faithfulness and righteousness, even though they did not yet have the answer to their prayer for a child.

Because of their faithful living, God chose them to be

the parents of a very special child. God chose Zachariah and Elizabeth to be the parents of John the Baptist–the forerunner and announcer of Jesus Christ to the World. Because God knew they would instill in that child an unswerving, unshakeable faith in God. Because having to wait on God's answer gave them the faithful experience to be able to teach John about waiting on the Lord. Because they did not give up on God, I believe that at just the right time he answered their earnest prayer in a remarkable way with a remarkable child.

God does have our best in mind. We live in a finite time and believe our prayers and petitions can only be answered in the way we think or want. But God's ways are not man's ways; his thoughts are not our thoughts. (Isaiah 55:8–9) We forget that God is not limited by the laws of nature. Everything about that first Christmas was about God doing the impossible. From the birth of John the Baptist to aged parents to the virgin birth of Jesus, God prepared Christmas exactly the way he needed it to be. God did the impossible at Christmas so that everyone would know Christmas was him.

But how do you tell an old man he is going to be a father when his years for fatherhood have long since past? First, you have to get him to the Temple. Then, you send the angel Gabriel.

Luke continues the story for us, beginning at verse 8.

"Now while on duty, serving as priest before God in the order of his division, As was the custom of the priesthood,

it fell to him by lot to enter [the sanctuary of] the temple of the Lord and burn incense. And all the throng of people were praying outside [in the court] at the hour of incense [burning]. And there appeared to him an angel of the Lord, standing at the right side of the altar of incense. And when Zachariah saw him, he was troubled, and fear took possession of him. But the angel said to him, Do not be afraid, Zachariah, because your petition was heard, and your wife Elizabeth will bear you a son, and you must call his name John [God is favorable]. And you shall have joy and exultant delight, and many will rejoice over his birth. For he will be great and distinguished in the sight of the Lord. And he must drink no wine nor strong drink, and he will be filled with and controlled by the Holy Spirit even and from his mother's womb. And he will turn back and cause to return many of the sons of Israel to the Lord their God. And he will [himself] go before Him in the spirit and power of Elijah, to turn back the hearts of the fathers to the children, and the disobedient and incredulous and unpersuadable to the wisdom of the upright [which is the knowledge and holy love of the will of God]–in order to make ready for the Lord a people [perfectly] prepared [in spirit, adjusted and disposed and placed in the right moral state]."

(LUKE 1:8-17 AMP)

Zachariah's time for his service at the Temple had come. He had left the hill country of Judea where he lived to go to Jerusalem. But of the priestly duties, one of the most sacred was to enter the Holy Place of the Temple and burn incense upon the Golden Altar of Incense.

This Altar stood in front of the veil that separated the Holy Place from the Most Holy Place. The Most Holy Place was where God's presence resided. In Solomon's Temple God's holy presence was above the Mercy Seat of the Ark of the Covenant. God commanded the priests to burn incense on the Golden Altar morning and evening as a symbol of the prayers of the people. The incense became a sweet smelling savor to God, as do our prayers today. It was a sacred duty to carry the prayers of the people before God. Offering incense on the Golden Altar was the closest a priest like Zachariah could get to the holy presence of God.

But which priest would go into the Holy Place to burn the incense? The answer came by casting lots: this time the lot fell to Zachariah. The honor to burn incense on the Golden Altar as an offering of the people's prayers may come once in a priest's lifetime. The lot fell to Zachariah and this day it was no coincidence.

And as Zachariah drew the lot that determined his priestly duties in the Temple that week, he had to be thrilled, amazed, and in awe all at the same time. He had been chosen by God to burn incense on the Golden Altar of Incense before the Veil of the Most Holy Place in the Temple.

Zachariah prepared the 4 sweet spices of stacte, onycha, galbanum, and pure frankincense that God had commanded to be burned as incense. (Exodus 30:34) He carefully measured out each one in accordance with God's instructions. He then took the incense and went to the Brazen Altar of Burnt Offering in the outer court of the Temple, just outside the Sanctuary of the Temple. From that Altar of Burnt Offering, Zachariah filled a censer full of burning coals of fire and carried it into the Holy Place. He placed the burning coals on the Golden Altar and laid the incense upon the coals to ignite the incense.

At that same moment, people had gathered outside the Sanctuary to offer up their silent prayers to God. They had been waiting until Zachariah had gone into the Holy Place with the incense and the coals. They had been watching to see when they could offer their prayers to God, believing that God was especially attuned to their prayers as he smelled the incense burning. The incense began to smolder and burn, sending up a column of smoke that filled the Holy Place with a sweet aroma of fragrance. I have to wonder if at this moment, as the smoke ascended as a symbol of prayer, Zachariah reminded God of his own unanswered prayer.

If Zachariah did, God had to smile, because God had already decided it was time to answer his prayer. God had already dispatched the angel Gabriel. Gabriel is God's special messenger, who stands in the presence of God in the throne room of Heaven. To Zachariah's surprise, the angel Gabriel appeared to him.

Gabriel stood just to the right of the Altar of Incense. Gabriel delivered God's message of the impossible to Zachariah.

Don't be afraid, Zachariah. God has heard your prayers. Elizabeth will bear you a son. But he is not going to be just any ordinary little boy. This son will be named John and he will bring back many of the children of Israel to serve God. He will speak and move in the spirit of Elijah–one of the greatest prophets of Israel. His job is simple: to make ready a people prepared for the Lord.

What an exciting word from God. The delay in prayer was answered by God with a child who would, upon seeing Jesus, declare "Behold the Lamb of God which taketh away the sin of the World." (John 1:29 KJV) But Gabriel's word is not just that John would be the forerunner and evangelist of Christ. It is not just that their son would be a famous preacher to Israel in the manner of their greatest prophet Elijah. In payment for the years of delay in receiving this gift of a son, God declared that their boy would be "a joy and delight to you." (Luke 1:14 NIV)

God made sure Zachariah and Elizabeth would be filled with joy and delight. God doubly rewarded Zachariah and Elizabeth. Not only did John bring them joy (meaning *to boast in the goodness of God*), but also delight; he quite literally filled their home with the light of God's love. John was their gift of gladness from God. In his song of praise at John's birth, Zachariah testified that the redemption of man by the coming of the Messiah enables us to serve God without fear, in full faith, and to serve him in holiness and righteousness all of our days. Zachariah and Elizabeth knew this truth to be real; they saw it in the eyes of their little boy every day.

It was not a coincidence that Zachariah's lot fell to the duty of offering incense on the Altar of Incense in the Temple that week of his duties. The angel Gabriel confirmed it: God had heard Zachariah's prayers. He had heard the tear-stained prayers of Elizabeth and sent Gabriel to announce the news of the answered prayer.

Just like the smoke from the incense rose from the Altar symbolizing the prayers of his people as a sweet smelling savor, God hears our prayers too–every single one of them. And he sends an answer every time. Sometimes the answer is just: "Not yet." The real question for us though is not whether the answer is yes, no, or not yet. It is: what are you going to do with that answer?

When the answer to your prayer finally comes, do you believe God? Zachariah had a problem here. Zachariah and Elizabeth had prayed for a child all of their lives, yet she was barren. Now they are old and well beyond childbearing years.

Then, when it is humanly impossible to bear a child, God sends Gabriel to announce the answer to their prayers. It is here that we see the humanness of Zachariah. Zachariah shows a little doubt. "How can I be sure of this? I am an old man and my wife is well along in years." (Luke 1:18 NIV) Zachariah is asking for proof.

Wait a minute, Zachariah. God just sent an angel to appear

to you and deliver the news. An angel! He is standing right in front of you! And God didn't send just any angel. He sent Gabriel, the messenger who stands before the presence of God. All these years you have lived out your faith, trusting God even though you couldn't explain it, and now you decide to doubt? Now you want to see proof? Watch how Luke describes Gabriel's response.

> *"The angel answered, 'I am Gabriel. I stand in the presence of God, and I have been sent to speak to you and to tell you this good news. And now you will be silent and not able to speak until the day this happens, because you did not believe my words, which will come true at their proper time.'"*
>
> (Luke 1:19-20 NIV)

Because Zachariah did not believe Gabriel's words were from God, Zachariah was stopped from speaking for nine months. I don't think Zachariah doubted God. I think he doubted that Gabriel was saying what God had told him to say. He was seeking proof that the message was true. After all these years, Zachariah just could not believe that now was the time. He couldn't fathom that God would wait all this time until now to answer their prayer. Gabriel must have gotten the message wrong. In that context, Gabriel said in effect: *Okay, if you don't believe what **I** am speaking to you is from God, then **you** won't be able to speak until John is born. That is how you will know. That is how you can be sure that what I've said is from God.*

But not being able to speak was an important sign. There has been no prophet of God to the children of Israel for over four hundred years! No human voice has been directly appointed to speak for God for centuries. Zachariah's silence reminded the people of God's silence for the past four hundred years. Zachariah's inability to speak for those nine months became a sign to the people that God was preparing to do something great.

It was also a sign to Elizabeth that God is about to do the miraculous in an old woman, just like he did for Abraham's wife Sarah—a miracle child was about to be borne by her. It was a sign to Zachariah's faith—don't doubt God's word.

God doesn't mind questions. God doesn't even mind questions about unanswered prayer. But God does not like our doubt. Doubt renders faith impotent. Doubt opens the door for fear to come in. Doubt tells God, I don't think you can. Zachariah is looking at the natural state of his world, he and Elizabeth are old and well past natural childbearing years. If this were to happen it would have to be a miracle from God.

Exactly! That is what God intended. That is God's plan. John is special. John's birth is a miracle. His conception is a sign to Mary that all things are possible with God, even the virgin birth. He has a vital and unique role to play in Christmas.

John couldn't be born in the ordinary course of things when Zachariah and Elizabeth were young. There would be nothing special about that, and his message might be interpreted as just his own concoction of thought. Being the forerunner of the

Messiah was vitally important. God wanted his people to know his silence was broken and Jesus was his message to them. God did not want his people to think it was a mere coincidence.

No, John had to be born when Zachariah and Elizabeth were way past natural. That put them in super-natural territory. Faith territory. Now, everyone takes notice that John is special. God does this so everyone will know John has been appointed by him.

The last words man had heard from God's servant were these: "He will turn the hearts of the fathers to their children and the hearts of the children to their fathers or else I will come and strike the land with a curse." (Malachi 4:6 NIV) That was the mission of Elijah in the Old Testament. And God, through Gabriel, announces to Zachariah that John the Baptist's role will be the same: "And he will go on before the Lord, in the spirit and power of Elijah, to turn the hearts of the father's to their children and the disobedient to the wisdom of the righteous–to make ready a people prepared for the Lord." (Luke 1:17 NIV)

God had specifically chosen Zachariah and Elizabeth to be the parents of this special boy. God repaid their difficult life with joy and delight. (Luke 1:14) And just as Gabriel said, the neighbors came when the boy was born and "shared her joy." (Luke 1:58 NIV) Everyone rejoiced.

When it came time to give the boy a name, both Elizabeth and Zachariah declared the name Gabriel had announced: John. At that moment, Zachariah's tongue was loosed and he could talk again. His first words were to praise God. He sang an entire song praising God. (Luke 1:67–79) The people, not only in Zachariah's town but throughout all of the hill country of Judea, heard about John's birth and the expectation for Christmas began: "What then is this child going to be? For the Lord's hand was with him." (Luke 1:66 NIV)

What are you expecting for Christmas? God gives every expectant mother time to prepare her heart and home for the arrival of her baby. There are joy and tears, work and pain, preparation and expectation. But it is the expectation that is the best. It is the hope of unlimited potential. Likewise, we should take the time to prepare for Christmas in our hearts and homes. We must also realize that one of the keys to Christmas spirit is found in taking time to expect the coming of Christmas. Make time to just sit and get excited about Christmas. Remember, joy is really about your ability to boast in the goodness of God in your life. Think back to all of the times God has shown up in your life and done something wonderful. What are you expecting for Christmas?

CHAPTER 12

JUST BELIEVE

What are the odds of Christmas even first occurring? What are the odds that a baby would be born in Bethlehem, wrapped in swaddling clothes and placed in a manger? For centuries, theologians and mathematicians have studied the Old Testament prophesies calculating the numerical likelihood of the coming of Jesus, the Messiah.

In the late 1800s, Dr. A.T. Pierson, a contemporary of the theological giants Scofield, Spurgeon, and Moody, considered over 300 of the distinct prophecies concerning the coming of the Messiah and calculated the probability of each and every one of those prophecies coming true in one person, in one place, at one point in time. He concluded that the odds of all of these prophecies occurring in one person were one chance in eighty-four–followed by nearly 100 zeros. In other words, the probability of one man fulfilling all of these prophesies at the same time in the same place is so improbable, so implausible, so incredible that it is humanly impossible. But if it did happen, that event would have to be the greatest occurrence mankind had ever seen. It could only be done by God. Since Jesus' life is a historical fact, there must be something to this story worth believing.

Yet for all those prophetic words to come true in one man is almost too impossible to believe. And Isaiah's prophecy that a virgin would conceive and bring forth a son is not some incalculable probability, it is to mankind a complete impossibility. But as Gabriel told Mary, nothing is impossible with God.

Here, at the crossroad of impossible with man and possible with God, is where faith must step in. When it comes to Christmas, we are not just believing what is possible in the natural, but we are also believing what is possible in God's supernatural. Believing, then, is really the point of the spirit of Christmas. To obtain the spirit of Christmas, you first must believe there was a Christmas–you must believe there was the first coming of Christ into this world.

It is not enough though to just believe in Christmas; we must also believe in the Christ of Christmas. It is not enough to just believe that a baby was born, wrapped in swaddling clothes, and placed in a manger so long ago. We must believe that baby was Jesus Christ. We must believe he is who he said he is. He is the Christ, the anointed one. He is the Messiah. He is the Savior come to redeem man from sin. He is the Son of God.

We must believe that Jesus came for the reason he said. The

Holy Spirit of God anointed Jesus to preach the good news of the gospel to the poor, to heal the brokenhearted, to preach deliverance to the captives, recovery of sight to the blind, and liberty to the bruised. (Isaiah 61:1–2; Luke 7:18) Jesus came that we might cast off the death-judgment of sin that we drag like Jacob Marley's chains behind our lives. He came to seek and to save those who are lost in their sin and have no way to escape. (Luke 19:10) He offers that escape from sin with the newness of eternal life; free from our sinful past.

We must believe that he did what he said and will do what he promises. Jesus is the only one who has lived a perfect, sinless life in the flesh; tempted in every fashion as we are yet without sin. He willingly sacrificed that life on a cross of death, taking our sin and shame upon himself. (1 Peter 2:24) And then Jesus was resurrected back to life by God the Father on Easter Sunday and lives forever. When we acknowledge he is the Savior, when we believe he died for our sins, when we put our whole faith in him by confessing our sins and accepting his forgiveness, then and only then have we truly believed in the Christ of Christmas. He promised: if we ask and confess, he will forgive and we will be clean from all of the unrighteous sinful acts of our past. (I John 1:9)

But putting our whole faith and trust in Jesus is difficult for some to do. They cannot believe what they cannot see with their eyes. Yet miracles happen all around us; we just lack the faith to see them clearly.

When our ability to believe lacks faith, the Bible steps in to provide us with an example onto which we can place our faith. The gospel writers Matthew, Mark, and Luke all record one such faith-building story. They relate the story of Jairus and his daughter. Though it is not part of the Christmas story, when we view this account as seen through the eyes of Matthew and through the insight of Luke and Mark, we will find the faith to believe in the Christ of Christmas.

The story of Jairus and his daughter is revealed to us in three scenes. Here is the first scene, as described by Luke.

> *"And it came to pass, that, when Jesus was returned, the people gladly received him: for they were all waiting for him. And, behold, there came a man named Jairus, and he was a ruler of the synagogue: and he fell down at Jesus' feet, and besought him that he would come into his house: For he had one only daughter about twelve years of age, and she lay a dying. But as he went the people thronged him."*
>
> (LUKE 8:40-42 KJV)

Jesus and the disciples have crossed back over the Sea of Galilee and have returned to Capernaum–on the northwest side of the Sea of Galilee–to the town from where they started the day before. The people had been waiting for Jesus to return. No doubt word had spread to the surrounding towns and villages and people had gathered, waiting for Jesus to return. So as the boat drew near the shore, Luke writes "the people gladly received him." (Luke 8:40 KJV)

Gladness, however, was not the scene in Jairus' house that day. His twelve-year-old daughter was dying. Luke records that she was his only daughter. Everything that could be done had been done, all to no avail. And I suspect that as he looked into the eyes of his dying little daughter and onto the face of his distraught wife, he knew of only one choice of action—he must find Jesus.

This may make sense to us, but for Jairus, this is a bold, radical step. It is action taken out of desperation. It is action taken without regard to the consequences. It is an action that only a father can understand. You see, in Capernaum everyone knows Jairus. He is the ruler of the synagogue in Capernaum. He is well known by all; he is respected. He is a man of affluence and a man of influence. He is a man of position and responsibility. He is a leader in the Jewish community of Capernaum.

So astonishing is Jairus' presence in the story that Luke exclaims: "behold, there came a man named Jairus, and he was a ruler of the synagogue...." (Luke 8:41 KJV) Why is this so astonishing for a ruler of the synagogue to seek out Jesus? People of his stature, people in his position in the religious community would not associate with Jesus. Jesus did not teach precepts that conformed to the belief system of the scribes and Pharisees. Jesus presented a message that the established religious community found threatening. Therefore, self-respecting Jews like Jairus would reject the teachings of this rabbi, Jesus.

Jairus was appointed by the elders of the synagogue in Capernaum to be the ruler of the synagogue. He held the respect of the elders in his community. He was responsible for the synagogue building and property upon which it sat. He was the general overseer of the public service on the Sabbath, including maintaining order (Luke 13:14). He would select the person who would read the Scripture and the person who would pray at each service.

If there were any visitors to the Sabbath service, Jairus would be the one to introduce them to the congregation and invite them to address the congregation or read Scripture. Because of the importance of the role and duties of the synagogue ruler, Jairus would have been a man of great affluence and influence in the community–synagogue life for the Jew was the center of community life for the Jew. He would have both experience and expertise in real estate management and leadership. Although a layman, he would have been a man devoted to Judaism. He was not a priest, rabbi, Pharisee, or scribe. But he was a man of position and prowess in the Jewish synagogue of Capernaum.

Luke points out Jairus' position as ruler of the synagogue because it is so important to this story. It tells us the desperation of the situation he faced. It tells us that although he was the ruler of the synagogue, he was willing to risk it all: his status, his prowess, his position, and his job to save his daughter.

It also tells us what Jairus may have seen, what he likely knew, and what he really believed. This story is a walk from religious formalism to faith in Christ. You see, Jairus would have been there the first day Jesus entered the synagogue in Capernaum. He would have introduced himself and took note that this teacher brought twelve of his disciples with him to service.

Jairus would have been the one to ask Jesus to read the Scripture and teach the Scripture lesson. As Mark records in his gospel, Jairus would have been in the synagogue that particular Sabbath, when Jesus taught so powerfully that the congregation was astonished, for this man "taught them as one that had authority, and not as the scribes." (Mark 1:22 KJV). Jairus had not heard the law and prophets taught like that before!

And he would have been there the day the demon-possessed man cried out in the middle of Jesus teaching, saying: "What do you want with us…. I know who you are–the Holy One of God!" (Luke 4:34 NIV) Jairus would have seen Jesus immediately command the unclean spirit to leave the man. He would have seen the unclean spirit come out and would have exclaimed with the congregation–"What a word this is! For with authority and power, he commands the unclean spirits, and they come out." (Luke 4:36 NKJV)

Jairus would have been in the synagogue when Jesus healed the man with the withered right hand on the Sabbath. (Luke 6:6–10). And Luke concludes the chapter by saying that the Pharisees and scribes were filled with madness–because they were there watching to see if Jesus would violate their twisted interpretation of working on the Sabbath and heal the man. Luke says they communed together to see what they could do to Jesus. I wonder, did they talk to Jairus? Judging from his actions, I believe Jairus began to doubt the efficacy of the theology of the Pharisees and scribes. How could they challenge a rabbi who did such miraculous works of God?

And I wonder if Jairus was also in the Capernaum house when the four friends lowered the paralytic man through the roof in front of Jesus. Remember how Mark recorded the story in Mark 2:1–12? The friends brought a paralytic man on a stretcher to the house where Jesus was teaching so that Jesus could heal their friend. But because of the crowd, they could not get in the door to get their friend to Jesus. These friends knew that if they could just get their paralyzed friend to Jesus, he would be healed. They believed. They had faith that was ready for action. Not dissuaded by the crowd in the house, they climbed up on the roof, lifted up their friend, tore off the roof to the house, and lowered their friend right down to Jesus. Mark then records, "When Jesus saw their faith, He said unto the paralytic, Son, your sins are forgiven you." (Mark 2:5 NKJV) Of course, that just set off the scribes, who didn't believe Jesus was the Son of God. They thought in their hearts: *this is blasphemy; who can forgive sins, but God alone?*

Jesus, immediately perceiving their thoughts, proclaimed to the crowd: Which is easier to say to this man? Is it easier to say your sins are forgiven or arise, take up your bed and walk? Watch this, then Jesus continues: So that you may know that the Son of Man has the power to forgive sins on earth, I'm going to say to this man who is paralyzed, Arise, take up your bed and walk. (Mark 2:10) And instantly the man is healed, takes up his bed, and walks out of the house. Mark then concludes: they were all amazed, glorified God, and said: *Well, we've never seen it like this before!* (Mark 2:12)

So why do I believe Jairus saw and heard all of these things? Look at what he did when he came to Jesus.

First, Jairus falls at Jesus' feet. (Exactly what the wise men did when they came to Jesus.) Only Matthew in his gospel account recognizes and records what Jairus did next: he began to worship. Notice, Jairus did not petition Jesus first; he did not present his plea. Even though his need was great and urgent, Jairus stopped and took time to humbly worship at Jesus' feet. We can benefit from Jairus' example: perhaps before we run down our list of needs and wants in our prayer time with God, we should likewise stop and spend the first moments just worshipping him for who he is.

Jairus has heard the teachings, he has seen the miracles with his own eyes. Jesus is a man who teaches with power and authority. He is not like the scribes or Pharisees. He does not teach powerless sermons like the other rabbis. The unclean spirit addressed Jesus as the Holy One of God. Jairus believes in who Jesus is! Though Jairus is a man of position and prowess, a ruler, leader, and man with authority, he humbles himself and falls at the feet of Jesus in adoration of the Holy One of God. Jairus looked on the face of Jesus; he looked into Jesus' eyes and saw the compassion and love of God. So, first Jairus humbly worships Jesus as the Holy One of God.

Second, listen to what Jairus said. Mark records his words. "My little daughter lies at the point of death. Come and lay your hands on her, that she may be healed, and she will live." (Mark 5:23 NKJV) You have to see the words in Greek to understand what Jairus believed in that moment. For the word "healed" in the King James Version, Mark uses the Greek word *sozo*. It can mean to heal, deliver, protect, but it is the also word which we translate to save. It literally carries the meaning that one is saved from death, perishing, or destruction by being healed. It's the same word Paul uses in Romans 10:9 to describe salvation. Paul says if we confess with our mouth the Lord Jesus and believe in our heart that God raised him from the dead, we shall be *sozo*. We shall be saved.

It is exactly what Jesus was saying when he healed the paralytic–your sins are forgiven (you are saved, *sozo*). And then to make the point clear–that Jesus had the power to both save and heal as God–Jesus healed the man with the command "Arise, take up your bed and walk."

I believe Jairus was in the house that day. He saw the paralytic man get out of his bed and walk. He heard Jesus declare that He has the power to forgive sins, to save and to heal. Jairus has made the connection that when Jesus saves he also has the power to heal. So he implores Jesus to save from death, to *sozo* his little girl. What Jairus needs now is for Jesus to come to his house, because Jairus believes Jesus is the Holy One of God who can save his daughter from death.

And what does Jesus do? Mark says "So Jesus went with him." (Mark 5:24 NKJV) I believe Jesus looked at Jairus and saw a ruler of the synagogue expressing faith in the Lord Jesus Christ. Jesus always responds to our exercise of faith. This is why faith is so important to our believing in the Christ of Christmas. When we exercise our faith to believe in Christ, Jesus responds by allowing the spirit of Christmas to be birthed in our hearts.

And that takes us to the second scene of this story. Jesus, Jairus, the Disciples and the multitude proceed toward Jairus' house. Here Mark picks up the story with insight and detail.

"And Jesus went with him; and a great crowd kept follow-ing Him and pressed Him from all sides [so as almost to suffocate Him]. And there was a woman who had a flow of blood for twelve years, And who had endured much suffer-ing under [the hands of] many physicians and had spent all that she had, and was no better but instead grew worse. She had heard the reports concerning Jesus, and she came up behind Him in the throng and touched His garment., For she kept saying, If I only touch His garment, I shall be restored to health. And immediately her flow of blood

was dried up at the source, and [suddenly] she felt in her body that she was healed of her [distressing] ailment. And Jesus, recognizing in Himself that the power proceeding from Him had gone forth, turned around immediately in the crowd and said, Who touched My clothes? And the disciples kept saying to Him, You see the crowd pressing hard around You from all sides, and You ask, Who Touched Me? Still He kept looking around to see her who had done it. But the woman, knowing what had been done for her, though alarmed and frightened and trembling, fell down before Him and told Him the whole truth. And He said to her, Daughter, your faith (your trust and confidence in Me, springing from faith in God) has restored you to health. Go in (into) peace and be continually healed and freed from your [distressing bodily] disease."

(Mark 5:24-34 AMP)

How far they had to travel to reach Jairus' house, we do not know. What the Gospel writers do reveal is that the multitude that had met Jesus at the seashore now followed him and thronged him. The press of the crowd was so great that the pace had to be slow. Even the disciples take note of the crowd thronging and touching Jesus along the way. (Mark 5:31) And while we can be sure Jairus was anxious and perhaps worried that Jesus may not get there in time, the next moment was orchestrated by God for the direct benefit of Jairus. A woman with a twelve-year issue of blood in her body is healed and Jesus stops the procession to hear her entire story. (Mark 5:30-34)

The seemingly untimely interruption of the woman with the issue of blood may appear to us as a delay in the story. I assure you it is not a delay. It is a divine pause for a divine purpose. Jesus knows exactly what he is going to do for Jairus–Jesus is going to meet the need Jairus will have, not the need he thinks he has. Jesus knows what we have need of, even before we ask. Jesus knows our future and is working everything for our good.

For Jairus, Jesus knows who is coming down the road next and the news they are carrying. Consider this: God loved Jairus so much, that on the very day his only daughter is born, he permits a woman to begin a twelve-year affliction with an issue of blood. This woman is specially chosen by God to fulfill a special need in one man's life twelve years in the future. He knows the path each life will take, and God knows the very point at which their paths will cross. It is all part of his plan. God has purposed this pause to build Jairus' faith, and when we apply its lesson to our lives, it will build our faith as well, especially in Christmas.

Understanding the purpose of the delay is learning the lesson. For every day that Jairus had been enjoying his new little girl, God had been preparing this dear woman for a faith-building lesson. God is standing at the intersection of this woman's desperate suffering and Jairus' desperate situation. Not every delay we encounter in our prayer life is a denial. Without this delay, without this woman's miracle of healing at this very moment,

Jairus' faith may have crumbled at the news his daughter–his only little girl–had died.

So there is an interruption on the way to Jairus' miracle; the woman secretly touches the hem of Jesus' garment with faith believing and is healed. Jesus stops the procession solely to bring this woman into sight. Up until that moment, only the woman and Jesus know what has happened. For her, the healing is the solution to twelve years of suffering. Jesus restores her physically, spiritually (her faith has saved her and made her whole/well), and socially (for Jesus restores the woman to society and tells her to go in peace–restored in relationship with man and God).

For Jairus, God intends to build his faith by seeing a miracle; by hearing the twelve-year story of this woman, her suffering, her spending all she had on doctors to no avail–all things Jairus had likely experienced with his sick daughter and could identify with. Then there is the healing and Jesus pronouncement: "And He said to her, Daughter, your faith has made you well. Go in peace, and be healed of your affliction." (Mark 5:34 NKJV) Her faith was the secret to her healing. She believed who Jesus was and she was made completely well, completely healed of her infirmity.

It is essential in God's plan (and necessary for Jairus' faith) that he hear and see this woman's act of faith and Jesus' confirmation of healing. The lesson for us: do not despise God-directed delays on the way to your miracle or answered prayer. Don't complain about the miracles in other people's lives while we suffer without a miracle in our life. Maybe God is building our faith through seeing the miracles in others. And this divinely purposed delay brings us to the third scene of the story.

Mark opens this third scene of the story at verse 35, which reads: "While he was still speaking, some came from the ruler of the synagogue's house who said, Your daughter is dead. Why trouble the Teacher any further? As soon as Jesus heard the word that was spoken, He said to the ruler of the synagogue, 'Do not be afraid, only believe.'" (Mark 5:35–36 NKJV) Here is the test of faith. This is the moment of decision: will he believe in Jesus?

The servants express the belief of the crowd–she's dead; there is nothing more that can be done. Perhaps, Jesus could have healed her had he gotten there in time, but it is too late. Even Jesus can do no more, so why bother him any further. I don't think this is because they did not want to believe. But up until this point in time, they had not seen a resurrection. Death was the end of their belief. The extent of their faith was in what they could possibly see, but not in the impossibility of what God can do.

But, watch what Jesus said. Jesus saw Jairus' faith by the seashore, so Jesus declares to Jairus–don't be afraid (alarmed or frightened) by what you have just heard. Keep on believing in me! And here is the insight for us. Notice that Jesus did not say, "Do not doubt". He said "Don't fear." Doubt is not the opposite of faith; doubt weakens our faith. Fear is the opposite of faith. Fear that God cannot or that God may not answer our prayer is what defeats our faith. God is not worried about your doubts–He is more than able to persuade you of who He is and what He can do. (Just ask King Nebuchadnezzar in Daniel Chapter 4!)

But when you fear, when you are frightened, that is when you stop believing. And what Jesus says is not *just believe*, that is, *just start believing*. Jesus is saying: *Believe like you did when you first came to me; believe like you did when you were worshiping at my feet, and keep on believing in me.*

Then Jesus does something that seems odd but has great spiritual significance. Mark records in verse 37 that Jesus permitted no one from the crowd to follow him, not even his disciples, except Peter, James, and John. He left all those who could only walk in the faith of what they saw to stay behind. The only ones who could go with Jesus and Jairus were those who believed in what they could not see. Their faith was a substance hoped for, the evidence of which they could not yet see. (Hebrews 11:1) But it would be seen! You had to have enough faith to believe that it would happen in order to go with Jesus.

And the lesson for us–when we pray or have need of a miracle, don't surround yourself with those who only can believe what they've seen. Leave the fearful and the faithless behind on the road. Move only with those who will join you to believe the impossible–for nothing is impossible with God. And if you can muster the faith to believe, all things are possible to those who believe. (Mark 9:23) When it comes to believing in the Christ of Christmas, where do you stand? Are you able to walk on in faith believing with Jesus or are you left standing on the road with the unbelieving crowd?

In the closing verses (38–43) of the chapter, Mark reveals the final part of this third scene to the story. Jesus comes to Jairus' house, and already the professional mourners have shown up. They are weeping and wailing and making a great fuss–as they are paid to do. It was common for well-to-do Jews to hire mourners when someone in the family died to show their great sorrow to the community. It became a status symbol of your riches–the more mourners you had, the more affluent and influential you must be. Clearly, Jairus had nothing to do with this–he had been with Jesus the entire time. I'm sure some relatives had spread the unfortunate news and arranged for the mourners.

Immediately, Jesus addresses the mourners and reveals a new understanding about death. *The damsel is not dead,* Jesus said, "She is just sleeping." Now, Jesus knew the girl was physically dead–but he was trying to make a point. When Jesus is in the house, death is like sleep. It is not final nor insurmountable for him. When we lie down for a nap, our spouse doesn't go into a panic and dial 911. It is the same faith-building moment for Jairus. Jesus wants him to know that when he couples his faith in what Jesus can do with his belief in who Jesus is and what he will do, his little girl's death is nothing more than sleep.

Of course, this upsets the professional mourners. First, they are not likely to get paid if the girl is actually just asleep. But they also know the truth – the girl is physically dead. So they laugh at Jesus. They have no faith and they are not there to believe in Jesus. They reject the possibility that Jesus can perform the miraculous and raise a girl from the dead just like waking a child from sleep. Second, they did not come to the house to see a miracle; they came to mourn.

And Mark records a phenomenal faith statement in verse 40: *"But when he had put them all out...."* (Mark 5:40 KJV) Jesus did not ask Peter, James or John to put them out. Jesus did it himself. I can just see Jesus taking them by the arm and showing them the door. Jesus put them out because their lack of faith, their inability to believe, was messing with the atmosphere in the house.

Why is atmosphere important? Consider how God created life. In Genesis 1 we see the pattern. First, God created light and he separated light from darkness. Then he created atmosphere. He separated the firmament of the heaven from that of the earth (literally separating the oxygen molecule from the H_2O water molecule to create atmosphere). Because without atmosphere, without air to breathe, there can be no human life. Jesus declares he is the Light of the world. (John 8:12) So when Jesus enters the house, light has entered. And when Jesus puts out the mourners, he has separated light from darkness. Now the atmosphere is right for life to occur.

Jesus takes the father, mother and his three disciples into the room where the dead girl lay. And Mark records some very precious words in verse 41. Jesus takes the girl by the hand and speaks in Aramaic: *Talitha cumi.* Mark interprets for us the words Jesus spoke: "Damsel, I say unto thee, arise." (Mark 5:41 KJV) But I think it loses something in the King James translation.

You have to remember what Jesus said he was doing. He was waking up a little girl from sleep. So just like a loving father would walk into the bedroom of his baby girl to wake her from a nap, Jesus gently takes her hand (so she will not be startled). She feels the warmth of his touch on her skin. He softly whispers Talitha…"Damsel," which really is a word of tenderness and endearment. So in our modern-day vernacular, I believe what Jesus really said is what any loving father would say to his baby girl: "Sweetheart, it's time to get up."

Instantly, the little girl woke from death and got up. Everyone is astonished. Jairus is overjoyed. The Holy One of God in whom Jairus had placed his faith was true and faithful. He had "saved" and healed his little girl! Then Jesus directs that something should be given the little girl to eat—just to prove to everyone this wasn't a ghost, but a real, live, breathing, eating little girl.

What has this story to do with the spirit of Christmas? The answer is found in the words Jesus spoke to Jairus: *Don't be afraid, just believe. Just believe in me.* Just believe in the Christ of Christmas. You may desperately want that true spirit of Christmas this year. But Christmas spirit will not come to you in the mere doing of Christmas activities. It is birthed in your heart when you believe in the Christ of Christmas.

The Christmas Spirit

So how do you capture the Christmas Spirit each December? How do you recover that child-like awe and anticipation of Christmas? Unlike Ebenezer Scrooge you do not need the terrifying visitation of three ghosts or the ghost of Jacob Marley. Just follow a few simple biblical principles taught by the lives of Mary, Joseph, the shepherds, the wise men and a few other people specially placed into the Christmas story. Following the keys presented in scripture will unlock the spirit of Christmas in your heart. Applying them to your life will bring Christmas spirit to you.

Christmas spirit comes when we *keep Christmas well.* Christmas spirit is that indescribable joy that emanates from deep within you. It starts when you accept Jesus into your heart and life. He brings the inexplicable peace that floods your soul and lifts your spirit. It is a peace that passes all understanding because he keeps you calm even though there may be chaos or confusion surrounding your everyday life. His presence in your life helps you keep Christmas well. He changes your heart which changes your attitude and you change your actions. He gives you a new life, a new outlook, a new hope, and a new reason to celebrate the Christmas season. The spirit of Christmas bubbles up from within you and puts a smile on your face and a spring in your step all year through. Because with Jesus on the inside, the real truth of Christmas is that its true spirit is a gift that can be carried with you and given to others throughout the year.

Christmas spirit comes when we *make room for Jesus in our heart, our home, for our children, and our church.* Renew the invitation of Jesus into your heart and home each Christmas. Let Jesus know that he is welcome to be a part of everything you do during the Christmas season. Be intentional in your plan to make Jesus the center of the celebration in your heart, home, and family. Be aware of those around you who like Mary and Joseph could use a little extra love this season. Share some of the bounty with which God has blessed you by giving to someone in need, whether extra Christmas cookies or a gift card. But it is not just the charitable foundations, find someone and make it a personal gift. It is in the giving that we receive the blessing of Christmas spirit.

Make room for Jesus in your Christmas decorations. Place a nativity scene on your front lawn (or on the door to your apartment) to tell your neighbors and all who pass by that Jesus has room in your home this Christmas. Add words like "believe", "faith", and "joy" to your decorations. Words have power because they enable the Holy Spirit to direct the attention of those who see them towards Jesus.

Make room for Jesus in your shopping and giving. It is easy to get caught up in the retailer's spirit of shopping and the world's concept of giving. God's gracious gift to mankind started Christmas. It was the gift of Jesus-the only begotten, one-of-a-kind perfect gift. We give because God gave. When we give to others we show not only that we care about them, but that they have value to us. God gave Jesus to us because we have value to him.

Make room for Jesus on Christmas morning. Pick the good news, gospel story of Jesus' first coming from either Matthew or Luke (or both). Reading his story is the best way to remind your family why we celebrate this season. Christmas is not just about decorations, gifts, and family: it's about the birth of Jesus Christ, our Savior and Lord.

Next, Christmas spirit comes when we *make a place for Christmas in our home.* Start by setting the atmosphere. Make room for Jesus in your decorating. Yes, Christmas decorations are important to lift our emotional spirit. There is nothing necessarily spiritual about the Christmas tree, garland or wreaths, but Christmas decorations cause us to suddenly focus on something out of our ordinary. It makes us focus on something important, real, and true. Christmas decorations do take time and energy, but they cause us to direct our attention to something worth celebrating-Jesus' first coming. And that puts our minds on a path towards Christmas spirit. So make Christmas visible in your home so it can be seen by you and by all who come to visit you.

But Christmas is not just in what is seen. Christmas is also in the sounds we hear. While there is no express statement that the Angels who visited the shepherds sang, we do know they praised God. And since Psalms 47:6-7 commands us to "Sing praises to God" I do not think it is a stretch of the imagination to believe that the angelic host broke forth into song. So be sure your home is filled with Christmas music that brings glory to God. When people visit your home at Christmas, they should be able to exclaim: *"This is a place where the spirit of Christmas is kept well!"*

Making your home a place that recognizes Christmas means you recognize Jesus has come. You understand it is about a time and place in history that Jesus first came. The key to Christmas spirit is remembering each day that he has come to take up residence in your life. He has come to be at home with you. When you accept Jesus into your heart you receive the Holy Spirit and you are now the temple of God. (1 Corinthians 3:16) Our homes should reflect that God dwells there, especially at Christmas because after all he is Immanuel, God with us.

Christmas spirit comes when we are *willing to be used of God.* Become a surrendered servant. Be a volunteer in your church and community; they need workers who are willing to give of their time. Volunteer at a nursing home to bring cheer to those who may have been forgotten by their families. Time is our most precious commodity–it is the one element that every person has exactly the same amount of each day. No one gets more, no one gets less. But how you spend that time speaks volumes about your priorities. Mary gave up all of her dreams and plans to follow the plan God had laid out before her. In return God gave her dreams and plans far beyond what she could have hoped for–she became the mother to the Son of God. Giving of ourselves is an easy way to bring Christmas spirit to our heart.

Christmas spirit comes when we *listen, obey, and do what God tells us.* Listen to the true voice of Christmas and do what he tells you to do. Be quick to obey his words and his instructions. Go beyond the witness and the wonder of Christmas and share your joy with others. Let those around you know that the real meaning of Christmas is found in accepting Jesus personally into your life.

Joseph was obedient to God's Word, which by implication meant he knew God's Word. Take time to read the Christmas story before Christmas day. Give yourself time to daily meditate on his word. God's promise for prosperity and success comes when we meditate on his Word. (Joshua 1:8) There is a framework, a structure built up in our lives when we read and apply God's Word to our lives each day. It gives us a solid foundation upon which to stand. Like the branches of a Christmas tree, knowledge of God's Word gives the Holy Spirit a place to hang opportunities to be the supply that meets the need of others.

On her own, Mary had no means to provide for a baby. So

God provided Joseph. He had a job, skill, and devotion to be the earthly father to Jesus and husband to Mary. So take time to study God's word. Take time to pray, asking the Holy Spirit to give you an opportunity to be a blessing to someone this Christmas. Be proactive about helping others. It may just be the kick-start your Christmas spirit needs.

Christmas spirit comes when you *share Jesus with others*. The key to receiving the joy the shepherds felt as they returned to their everyday lives, comes in sharing the good news of the gospel with others. You cannot keep a good story to yourself. You should not keep the good news of the gospel to yourself. The Christmas season makes it so easy to share the good news because everyone's mind is already thinking about it. God intended Christmas to be about him. The message is the same as it was for the shepherds. The Prince of Peace has come. Share that peace with others and watch the joy of Christmas blossom in your heart.

Christmas spirit comes if we *never lose the wonder*. Don't treat Christmas as the "same ole, same ole." It should not be treated as just another Christmas. It is not just another day on the calendar, and it is not just another holiday. Take time to wonder and be in awe of Christmas. Ponder why you are celebrating Christmas. Like Mary, ponder and give thought to why and how you are remembering Christ's coming.

Years ago, there was a dear saint of God at our church, Ms. Rose. She had a speech impediment that made talking difficult and understanding what she said even more difficult. For obvious reasons, she shied away from interactions with adults, but she loved children. Her ministry was the nursery because babies understood her love. In the nursery her words did not matter. The babies just heard the love of Jesus in her voice. But every Christmas, Ms. Rose brought a birthday cake to Church and had everyone sing *Happy Birthday* because it was Jesus' birthday. She did not want anyone to forget why we celebrate the Christmas season. Ms. Rose never lost the wonder. Accepting the wondrous gift of God with all of its wonder and awe is another key to Christmas spirit, and Ms. Rose kept Christmas well.

Christmas spirit comes when we are *willing to worship*. The magi focused on a star that lead them from observation to faith. The star God provided did not just lead them to a baby in a manger, but led it them to faith in God and faith in the son of God, the King of Kings.

We know they moved from intellect to faith, because they did something with their research, their observation, and their study. They brought gifts that spoke to Jesus' royalty, the purpose of his coming and the ministry of his life while here. They came to worship. That is what they told Herod. Worship is the key to unlock Christmas spirit. Be the worshipper that humbly falls before Jesus and acknowledges that he is the King of Kings and Lord of Lords. He is the Holy One of God. True Christmas spirit worships Jesus. (John 4:24)

Christmas spirit comes when we are *doing that needful thing.*

The key is figuring out what that needful thing is for you and your family and then doing that thing. It may be different for each of us, but it will involve letting go of the clutter and distraction that often accompanies Christmas. The irony about "time saving devices" is that the more we use them the less time we seemingly have. They seem to give us more reason to fill up our time, often with things that are not needful. Like Martha, our Christmas becomes cumbered with much doing.

The key to a lasting, look-forward-to-doing kind of Christmas is to focus on a tradition, memory or family experience that encourages everyone to celebrate Jesus. It is something that builds up our family. It is something that reminds us of how important our family is to each of us.

Although she was her sister, Mary was not Martha's servant. Mary was not called to hospitality ministry like Martha. But Mary does need to remember that Martha would always welcome her help. And Lazarus should not be left out. There are things he can do like washing the dishes after the meal. It is a simple task that will be greatly appreciated by the cook who has been on her feet all day preparing the Christmas feast. Find one needful thing and do it. It will make everyone's Christmas a blessed time with Jesus.

Christmas spirit comes when we remember *we are never too old for Christmas*. Christmas is not age dependent. Without Jesus, we will eventually be disappointed by the world's Santa Claus myth surrounding Christmas. But when we set our focus on Jesus we can find new joy to celebrate each year, no matter what our age. Like Simeon and Anna, we can find our purpose in being the witness to the redemption of man by the coming of the Messiah. If we allow ourselves to be guided and daily-directed by the Holy Spirit, we will become daily professors of the truth of God's word. It will be a spoken word that God can then reveal in the hearts of those who hear. To become the person God can use to declare his truth, we must be the daily seekers of God and daily speakers for God in this world. If you never let your age deter you from celebrating Christmas, you will be surrounded by others bringing their Christmas spirit too.

Christmas spirit comes when we are *expecting Christmas.* Things worth waiting for are things worth preparing for. Zachariah and Elizabeth did not allow the greatest disappointment of their lives deter them from serving God. In truth, their devotion and righteous living came because they chose to trust God, even if they could not fully understand God. And that trust was rewarded by the answer to the very prayer they thought long past possible.

But Christmas is about impossibilities. It is the time when we exercise our faith to believe. We must realize that Christmas spirit is found in taking time to expect the coming of Christmas. Make time to just sit and get excited about Christmas. Spread that expectation around to your family and friends. Remember that joy is really about your ability to boast in the goodness of

God in your life. God shows up with joy and delight when we take time to expect his arrival.

Finally, Christmas comes when we *just believe in the Christ of Christmas.* Christmas spirit comes when you move from knowing about him to kneeling before him. Jairus knew about Jesus—he had heard him teach, he had seen him heal, he had heard what was said of him. But the desperate need in his life—to find healing for his little girl—moved him to action. He put faith to his knowledge and knelt before Jesus, worshipping him for who he is.

Ultimately it is not the doing of Christmas that brings the joy, wonder, and awe of Christmas spirit. It is believing in the Christ of Christmas that brings Christmas spirit. And that believing will carry you through all year long, from Christmas to Christmas. Can you keep Christmas well?

References

Arekion, Dr. Glenn. 2018. "Sunday School Session - The nature of Old Testament sacrifices." Lanham, MD. January 14, 2018.

Betzer, Dan. 1982. *Revivaltime Radio Sermons - 1982.* Edited by Revivaltime Media Ministries. Springfield, Missouri: The General Council of the Assemblies of God.

Biblical Geographic. 2011. *Migdal Eder, Bethlehem, Israel.* September 28. www.biblicalgeographic.com.

Blomberg, Craig L. 1997. *Jesus and the Gospels.* Edited by John Landers. Nashville, Tennessee: Broadman & Holman Publishers.

Buehler, Dr. Juergen. 2012. *The Tower of the Flock.* November 22. https://int.icej.org/news/commentary/tower-flock.

Christenbury, Dr. Eugen C. 2001. *Evangelical Sunday School Lesson Commentary 2001-2002*. Edited by Lance Colkmire. Vol. Fiftieth Annual. Cleveland, Tennessee: Pathway Press.

Colkmire, Lance. 2008. *Evangelial Sunday School Lesson Commentary 2008-2009*. Edited by Lance Colkmire. Vols. Fifty-Seventh Annual. Cleveland, Tennessee: Pathway Press.

Dickens, Charles. 2006. *A Christmas Carol*. Cambridge, Massachusetts: Candlewick Press.

Dubose, Rev. Rick. 2017. "Plenary Session I." *Fathering The Next Generation - Washington Region Conference - Potomac Ministry Network*. Temple Hills, Maryland. Accessed March 18, 2017.

Faithlife Corporation. 2017. *Faithlife Study Bible*. Edited by John D. Barry. Lexham Press, May 17. Accessed July 2017. www.faithlife.com.

Hayford, Jack W., Sam Middlebrook, Jerry Horner, and Gary Matsdorf, . 1991. *Spirit Filled Life Bible - New King James Version*. Nashville: Thomas Nelson Publishers.

Henry, Matthew. 1996. *Matthew Henry's Commentary on the Whole Bible New Modern Edition.* Vol. 5. 6 vols. Hendrickson Publishers, Inc.

Life Publishers International. 1992. *The Full Life Study Bible - King James Version.* Grand Rapids, Michigan: The Zondervan Corporation.

—. 1992. *The Full Life Study Bible-New International Version.* Grand Rapids, Michigan: The Zondervan Corporation.

Mathews, Shailer. 1906-1918. *Betrothal.* Edited by James Hastings. Accessed July 6, 2017. http://wwwstudylight.org/dictionaries/hdn/b/betrothal.html.

Online Parallel Bible Project. 2016. *Biblehub.* www.biblehub.com.

Online Parallel Bible Project. 2004-2017. *Barne's Notes on the Bible (1834).* Accessed December 29, 2017. http://biblehub.com/commentaries/barnes/micah/4.htm.

Oxford University Press, Inc. 1967. *The New Scofield Reference Bible HOLY BIBLE Authorized King James Version.* Edited by C.I. Scofield. New York, New York: Oxford University Press, Inc.

Sand, Rhonda. 2016. *Tower of the Flock*. December 20. www.livingpassages.com.

The Zondervan Corporation and The Lockman Foundation. 1987. *The Amplified Bible*. Grand Rapids: Zondervan.

Vine, W.E., Merrill F. Unger, and William White, Jr. 1996. *Vine's Complete Expository Dictionary of Old and New Testament Words*. Nashville, Tennessee: Thomas Nelson, Inc.

About the Author

Ron Davis is an attorney, teacher, author, speaker, leader, husband, father, and student of the Bible (not necessarily in that order). Professionally, he is a practicing corporate attorney, having worked for the past 30 years in both private practice and as in-house corporate counsel. He holds a Juris Doctorate from American University and a Bachelor of Arts in political science and criminal justice from the University of Maryland. When not practicing law, Ron's passions are teaching an adult Sunday school class and leading the boys in the Royal Rangers group at his church. He has done both for over forty years. Ron is an energetic and entertaining speaker/story-teller on both professional and Bible topics. He is husband to Christie, his wife of over 33 years and father to their 4 twenty-something aged kids: twin daughters and two sons. They live in the suburbs outside Washington, D.C., with their schnauzer/cocker spaniel, named Lincoln.